T0163372

FINDING STILLNESS IN A NOISY WORLD

FINDING

STILLNESS

IN A

NOISY

WORLD

JANA RICHMAN

THE UNIVERSITY OF UTAH PRESS
Salt Lake City

Copyright © 2018 by The University of Utah Press. All rights reserved.

 The Defiance House Man colophon is a registered trademark of
The University of Utah Press. It is based on a four-foot-tall Ancient
Puebloan pictograph (late PIII) near Glen Canyon, Utah.

LIBRARY OF CONGRESS CATALOGING-IN-PUBLICATION DATA
Names: Richman, Jana, 1956- author.
Title: Finding stillness in a noisy world / Jana Richman.
Description: Salt Lake City : The University of Utah Press, [2018] |
   Identifiers: LCCN 2017060285 (print) | LCCN 2017061596 (ebook) | ISBN
   9781607816270 (ebook) | ISBN 9781607816263 (pbk.)
Classification: LCC PS3618.I348 (ebook) | LCC PS3618.I348 A6 2018 (print) |
   DDC 813/.6--dc23
LC record available at https://lccn.loc.gov/2017060285

An excerpt of "The Land of No Use" appeared in *Red Rock Stories*, Torrey
House Press (2017).

"A Desert beyond Fear" appeared in the *New York Times* (2012).

"Stay" appeared in the *Fourth River* (2016).

"The Curling Fingers of the Hatch Women" appeared in *Utah Reflections:
Stories from the Wasatch Front*, The History Press (2014).

"Wild Thoughts" appeared in *Comeback Wolves*, Johnson Books (2005).

"The Sharp Points" appeared in *15 Bytes* (2016).

"Moving Water" appeared in *Desert Water: The Future of Utah's Water Resources*,
University of Utah Press (2014).

"Dirt Fantasies" appeared in *Dirt: A Love Story*, University Press of New
England (2015).

"Dark Love" appeared in *Nature, Love, Medicine*, Torrey House Press (2017).

Printed and bound in the United States of America.

For Steve Defa, my partner in stillness

CONTENTS

ACKNOWLEDGMENTS

The noise of the world seems to increase with each passing year, while my tolerance for it decreases. We are told to "make our voices heard," which eventually, in my experience, results in a deafening roar with no recognizable message. Instead of insisting on being heard, what if we all sat in stillness for a while? What, one wonders, would be the result of that?

Each of the essays in this collection, in its own way, demanded stillness from me. I thank those who provided me with space and silence in the physical sense: M. B. and Chuck McAfee who bigheartedly offered me the great gift of time spent at their sweet cabin on the Dolores River, and the generous founders and staff—particularly Deb Ford—of Playa Artist Residency, a desert sanctuary.

I thank those who provided me with the opportunity for solitude in a hundred small ways that add up to long stretches of time: my clan in the community of Escalante, Utah, the members of which continue to let me know that I am welcome at any social gathering even after I've declined 99 percent of them; my bosses and colleagues at eLearning Innovation who believe that work is work and life is life, and a life should be filled with more than work; and the activists who fight tirelessly for open space where stillness endures—however vulnerably—because they know humans cannot thrive without it.

Many thanks to fellow writers Dorothee Kocks, Jane Gerhard, Amie Tullius, Melanie Bishop, Steve Trimble, Thomas Lowe Fleischner, and Barbara K. Richardson for being wise and conscientious readers of this work and responding with advice, encouragement, good company, wisdom, food, editing, and friendship.

Thanks to John Alley for his steady direction and editing adroitness, and to John and others at the University of Utah Press for the knowledge and care brought to bear on this and every book they publish.

To Doug Stewart, my agent, who has never been anything but kind, wise, and generous with his guidance, I owe a great debt of gratitude.

As always I thank Steve Defa for believing in the sanctity of solitude and the power of stillness but mostly for knowing that writing is part of my soul's code.

PREFACE

My first real love was an anthropomorphized pig named Wilbur who shared his pigpen with his wise and loyal friend Charlotte. I identified strongly with Wilbur, a pathetic runt prone to self-pity and easily moved to blubbering hysterics. Wilbur and I spent our early years in much the same manner: desperate for friends, shunned by barnyard animals, and seeking fun, frolic, and warm straw into which we could burrow knowing we were safe and loved. Our search for such an existence gave purpose to our lives.

Charlotte's Web was first published in 1952, four years before I was born. In my memory, I got the book in first grade, although upon reading *Charlotte's Web* as an adult, the book seems too sophisticated for someone in her Dick and Jane years, and I was not a precocious child by any measure. Nonetheless, I cling to the memory of discovering Wilbur early and holding him close throughout my grade-school years.

My next real love was Wilbur's creator. E. B. White was the humorous, storytelling father I never had. I gaze at pictures of him, each one of them sporting the face—and often the suit coat if not the necktie—of the stern but fair father, his quick wit cloaked by his ubiquitous civility.

Nearly thirty years would pass between my childhood discovery of White and my adult rediscovery of him. During that time, I engaged in the necessary stumbles of life. I flunked out of college, became a bride at 17 and a divorcee soon thereafter, went back to college, became an accountant, made money, lost money, quit counting, married again, and divorced again before

I came upon White's work when a professor recommended *The Elements of Style* to make up for my spotty education in the basics of good writing. But it wasn't until just past my fortieth birthday, when in a graduate writing program I was assigned to read White's essay "Once More to the Lake," that I began to grasp the quiet magnificence of White's work. Since then, I have kept him close, always turning to his essays when I need a dose of humanity, humor, and good sense.

Starting in 1938 and continuing until 1943, White published a monthly piece in *Harper's Magazine* under the heading "One Man's Meat," and in 1942, a collection of essays under the same title, which was expanded in 1944. I found a tattered 1944 edition of *One Man's Meat* on a dusty shelf in a used-books store next to four other volumes of White's work. I bought them all and wrote my name inside the front covers, a show of permanence. The 1944 edition of *One Man's Meat* is now covered with yellowing tape as I attempt to keep it together for as long as I, myself, manage to stay together.

My working title for this collection of essays was *One Woman's Meat*. I borrowed White's title with reverence, trusting that White may have found humor in the dubious honor. If I were a good enough writer to steal more from White than his title—his spot-on prose or his keen observance of human dilemma—I would not hesitate, but, alas, I'm limited by my own deficiencies. I borrowed White's title as motivation for clean prose and grammatical correctness, both apt to fall short of their mark.

In the foreword of my edition of *One Man's Meat,* White describes the collection of essays as "a personal record...which I wrote from a salt water farm in Maine while engaged in trivial, peaceable pursuits, knowing all the time that the world hadn't arranged any true peace or granted anyone the privilege of indulging himself for long in trivialities."

That seems a perfect description of what I have collected here: a personal record written from a small shed set under the "junk trees" on my town parcel in Southern Utah while engaged in trivial and usually peaceable pursuits. Though I hear nothing from my shed at the moment but the singsong of crickets and an occasional complaint from a dog disturbed by one of fewer than eight hundred people or one of more than eight hundred skunks in town, I'm not fooled into thinking the world has arranged any truer peace now than it had in 1938 when White began the essays later published as *One Man's Meat*.

Of course White's essays were far more than a personal record and the "personal" part of that description is a stretch. The essays of *One Man's Meat* are also significantly more than a historic record. White's insights transcend both time and place, and many of his observations have, as he once put it, "the odor of durability to them."

In July of 1938, in an essay entitled "Removal," White observed the nation's growing affection for the latest technological invention—television—and lamented that "sound 'effects' are taking the place once enjoyed by sound itself...and television sights may become more familiar to us than their originals." White feared that we would "forget the primary and the near in favor of the secondary and the remote." As the dead-on accuracy of White's misgivings fade without notice into our collective consciousness, I immerse myself in his words, knowing that he's speaking directly to me, believing that as he and his "vile old dachshund, Fred," throw slop to the pig, they do so with a hint of disconcertion for my welfare in this time and place.

I too, like White, made the choice to permanently leave a city, for which I have a great fondness, in favor of a rural locale. It was not a moral choice—I hold no judgments on the ability of one place over the other to infuse a life with spiritual enlightenment—only a personal preference. Unlike White, I grew up with the smell of cow manure in my nostrils and hay leaves in my underwear and with a singular meaning attached to the phrase "going to the store."

I held no romantic notions of rural life. I knew I would be witness to the anguish of dogs permanently attached to the ends of chains, earwigs in my kitchen cupboards, and flies in numbers only horse manure can produce, all of which I am asked to accept with as little comment as possible. Nor do I place myself in any loftier position having come from the city than those who were smart enough to stay put from the get-go.

Nine years into the decision to move to Escalante, the romance remains at bay. But something here stirs me. Something has burrowed in and created a discernible track through my interior terrain as conspicuous—and maybe as arbitrary—as the gopher trails running through the yard. This collection of essays is my attempt to figure out what this place has done to me.

Once I left my hometown of Tooele, Utah, in the early '80s, I spent many years running from Utah's west desert, a place that had trapped the awkwardness and pain of my adolescence in its arid severity. The west desert held the yearning part of me, the part that could never be mollified because its object eluded me.

One evening in a Salt Lake City reading group discussion of Julie Otsuka's novel *When the Emperor was Divine,* the setting for which is the Topaz Internment Camp in Utah's west desert, the conversation turned to the dreadfulness of the place—not the camp but the desert itself—and all generally agreed that a more horrifying geographic location could not be found. I made a comment that Utah's west desert has been—and continues to be—devastated by ATVs and the military, and the response from one and all was, "Who cares?" Evidently I do. My defenses escalated and tears trickled, although I had been asking myself the same thing for years. Who cares? I hadn't driven in quite some time any farther than the west end of Vine Street in Tooele, where my parents still lived, busy as I was transforming myself into a city girl, but apparently the west desert still had hold of me.

The next day I drove past Great Salt Lake, around the north tip of the Oquirrh mountain range, through Tooele, and past Settlement Canyon Dam. I continued through Stockton and Rush Valley and over Johnson's Pass on Highway 199, threading my way between the Onaqui and Stansbury Mountains. When the guard gate of Dugway Proving Grounds appeared, I took a left off the pavement onto the Pony Express Trail and stopped at Simpson Springs, a place familiar to me from high-school keg parties. There I spent the day alternating between joy—derived from sheer beauty and solitude—and sadness resulting from the same.

Entering the west desert is to rake the rawness of the most sensitive spot I carry. Everyone has one, a tender place inside—the place of the child, the place of loneliness and vulnerability. That's the west desert. It never gets old; it never gets easy; it never stops breaking my heart. Driving into it, walking through it, sitting on the side of a gravel road to watch a band of wild horses graze gives me a simultaneous rush of peace and sorrow. Tears of solace and tears of regret flow in unison.

When my husband and I decided to leave the city, we were both seeking open desert for reasons that were not clear to me before I wrote the essays in this collection. We considered the west desert, but in the end, it proved too provocative for me. I was afraid it would peck at me incessantly, like a raven on roadkill. The deserts and canyons of the Escalante felt softer. A paradox. I thought the sandstone canyons that had been torn, gashed, and lacerated by wind and water over millions of years might hold tranquility in their dark caverns. That turned out to be true, but they don't offer it up freely.

Whenever I visit a city now, I come home feeling like I've been on a bender. I feel a little grubby and a little obscene after getting swept up in the city's consumption and excess. From Salt Lake City, it takes me four and a half hours to reach the edge of the Hogsback on Highway 12, and there, where the land drops off both sides of the road and sweeps wide with Navajo Sandstone and Kayenta Formation, I loosen my grip on the wheel, exhale, and come back to myself. I'm home.

When I highlight "desert" in Microsoft Word and click on the handy Thesaurus and Dictionary function—certainly not an exhaustive or authoritative source but one that represents mainstream thinking—the following terms pop up: Wasteland. Deprived place. Lifeless place. Barren region. Desolate tract. If I open *The Synonym Finder* I can add: Dust bowl. No man's land. Devoid. Empty. Destitute. Poor. Deficient. Uncultivable. Unproductive.

We believe these words. They are part of our American sensibilities, part of our consciousness. They are what allowed the

Mormons to make Utah's desert "bloom like a rose." They are what drive us to cover deserts with malls and golf courses and lawns.

It is easier to hide from oneself in the city than it is in an open desert, much easier to distract oneself from whatever pain or shame or fear flows just under the skin. A desert will confront a person, which might be why we treat them so shabbily, refuse to let them be, rush to cover them with concrete and roses.

The day after I return home from the city, I drive the *desolate tract* called Hole-in-the-Rock Road to the *barren region* known as Harris Wash. From there I walk several miles through the *wasteland* of flowing pink sand, pinyon pine, juniper, sage, and wheatgrass before settling into the *lifeless place* between soaring rust-red sandstone walls and a cornflower-blue sky.

The essays in this collection reflect the confrontational and brutal nature of the desert. They also reflect its openheartedness, its trust, its embracing nature. The interconnectedness of those seemingly incongruous temperaments is significant. It is that tryst that tunnels into a person, scrabbles around, and rearranges things until it finds a place to nestle.

The essays in this collection can be read in any order, one at a time or as a group, but they are, with a few exceptions, presented in the order in which they were written. If read in this order, the subtle burrowing nature of the exterior into the interior becomes apparent—at least it finally became apparent to me.

THE LAND OF NO USE

*It is a wholesome and necessary thing for us to turn
again to the earth and in the contemplation of her
beauties to know of wonder and humility.*

—Rachel Carson

When the weather allows it, I ride my bike to the post office
to gather mail and read town announcements on the bulletin
board. Most of the mail goes directly from cubbyhole to garbage—the important stuff is on the board: feral cat trapping
and neutering on Thursday; mammogram mobile in front of
old gym on Monday; irrigation at 50 percent; ban on ditch and
weed burning until further notice; watermelon bust in the park
on Saturday, all welcome. Those who are truly welcome know
who they are; those who are not also know it.

As I pass my neighbor's house on the way to the post office,
I take note of the bumper sticker on the back of his pickup
truck: *Wilderness: The Land of No Use.* My neighbor and I disagree on this sentiment and, I suppose, many others. When he
sees me, he smiles and waves, and I do the same. I don't know
his philosophy of life beyond his bumper sticker, but I make
assumptions. He does the same about me. I know through
other means of communication that he does not like living in
close proximity to me. I am an interloper in *his* town. He may
be surprised to know that I empathize with him.

Our lives are often driven by a desire to hold tight to what we have or to recapture something we've lost. We call it nostalgia and try to dismiss it with a shrug and a wave, but it can linger and deepen and turn sour.

My earliest memories of my own rural Utah hometown include Swan's Grocery, a two–cash register, raw meat–smelling, family-run establishment soothingly similar to Griffin's Grocery in Escalante. In fewer than thirty years, Swan's was replaced by Allen's Foodtown, which was replaced by Albertsons, which was replaced by Smith's, which was joined and dwarfed by Walmart Supercenter. My town of open ditches, wild wheat fields, Bevan's Drugstore, and the Ritz Hair Salon disappeared. Fast food, chain pharmacies, parking lots, and strangers created a different town with the same name.

The loss felt personal and abrupt. The town didn't die naturally; it was murdered, trampled to death. And I was bitter toward the newcomers, the careless crushers of my childhood, the smiling slaughterers lining the fresh pavement of McDonald's drive-thru and squeezing into new vinyl booths at Applebee's.

Looking to mitigate the internal damage, I fled my hometown for an urban life, thinking, mistakenly, that because cities have already covered the earth's natural surface, a similar loss could not be experienced there. I went first to Salt Lake City, then to New York City, then to Tucson, Arizona. But time has a way of not only catching up to, but rolling over me. Either my essential nature moves more slowly than that of my fellow human, or my fellow humans have a means for adjustment that eludes me, and one day I awaken to the small, familiar stone in my belly warning me that things are amiss, that the place I'm occupying is changing faster than I can adapt, and I will soon be out of synch with my location.

I left Tucson as the city began to consume itself, to feed on its own entrails as it crawled through and devoured the Sonoran Desert. I returned to Utah, acknowledging that it is my place, the only place I've ever called home. I settled in Salt Lake City determined to find a way to be okay with, or oblivious to, change and loss. I failed. I would leave Salt Lake City in the same way: mourning the loss of downtown department stores to malls, the loss of foothills to development, the loss of mountain solitude to "multiple use," and ultimately a loss that became irreconcilable: breathable air.

Without knowing how we would support ourselves, my husband and I came to Escalante. We moved into a house reeking of cat urine, tore out carpets, scrubbed the plywood underneath, and scattered throw rugs. We chose Escalante because it appeared to be a town that had somehow held onto itself over the last hundred years of exponential population growth and insidious technology—two things that I struggle and often fail to embrace.

The first night, unable to tolerate the stench of Clorox-cloaked urine, we built a small bonfire in the backyard and sat near it on stumps. One might think we would question our decision at that point, question what we were running from and running to, but we never did. Staring into the flames, with one simple breath, I let go of the persistent feeling of placelessness that I hadn't realized I'd been carrying since 1974. We knew this to be our final move.

Scenic Byway 12, the only way in or out of Escalante on pavement, winds its way through Red Canyon, past Bryce National Park, through Grand Staircase-Escalante National Monument, over Boulder Mountain on the Aquarius Plateau, and ends close to Capital Reef National Park. The road is 124 miles long and remains true to its name: It is spectacularly scenic. Escalante sits at the midway point, surrounded on three sides by the Monument, the fourth occupied by pine and aspen forest of the Aquarius Plateau. Grand Staircase-Escalante National Monument, made up of about 1.9 million acres, is by no stretch of the imagination "wilderness," but it is a nice piece of property.

If you drive in from the west, you would be guided by Powell Point, a ten-thousand-foot, jagged hunk of pink, red, lavender, or orange limestone—depending upon the passing clouds and changing light—with a rim of white around its peak from which you can look down upon "the blues," rolling hills of shale deposited eighty million years ago by an inland ocean.

From the east, you would travel the Hogsback, a suitably named narrow strip of pavement slapped down on an equally thin ribbon of rock. On either side, the earth abruptly spills to slickrock canyons below. From the Hogsback the canyons tease with winding slivers of greenery, but they don't reveal their secrets. They hide their creeks and waterfalls and swimming holes, their Indian art panels and ruins and dinosaur bones, their songbirds and wild turkeys and mountain lions, their sandy washes and red-walled slots from anyone not willing or able to travel on foot. They care not about accessibility, equality, or opportunity.

No matter the direction, when you drive across the land to get to Escalante, you must acknowledge the exposed and ancient vulnerability of the earth; you must recognize the authority of wind and water and time; you must concede human lowliness. Or you must narrow the scope of your mind to prohibit such thoughts.

*

I leave my pink bike unchained and unattended next to the post office planter box filled with daffodils in early spring and tomato plants in late summer. Ryan, our postal employee, greets me by name as he does everyone who walks through the door. Still, I often feel jittery going into the post office—not because I think someone will steal my bike but because the post office serves as the town gauge. It carries the volatile emotions of its residents as honestly as a child.

Escalante is divided, not quite equally, between "locals" and "move-ins," most commonly split down religious lines: Mormon and non-Mormon respectively. The Mormons were by no means the first humans in the canyons of the Escalante—evidence of earlier clans can be seen on walls and ledges—but they lay claim to the place nonetheless. They settled the town in 1875 and operated as a mostly closed society for more than six generations. That has changed in recent years, and my neighbor is not the only one unhappy about it. If you don't believe me, visit the post office.

A while back, the man who was Escalante's mayor made his first trip to Washington, D.C., to appear in front of the Congressional Subcommittee on National Parks, Forests, and Public Lands. Rumor had it that he was nervous during his debut on the national stage, but he managed to summarize our town's woes and place the blame for them at the foot of the federal government—specifically the nicely shined, Italian leather shoes of former President Bill Clinton, who in 1996 created Grand Staircase-Escalante National Monument.

The mayor spoke of the "devastating social and economic impact" on Escalante caused by the creation of the monument. He cited a lack of jobs, a decrease in per capita income, an unstable town economy relying on tourism, floundering schools facing the possibility of closure, and young families moving away. The mayor's performance was followed by that of a representative from the nonprofit research group Headwaters Economics, who painted the opposite picture in equally broad strokes—more jobs, an increase in per capita income, and a thriving tourism economy—attributed to the creation of the monument.

The mayor's comments reignited the latent tension that runs a jagged line through the locals and move-ins and gives the town its reputation as a crabby little place, a distinction we simultaneously abhor and cherish. The locals were proud of their mayor; the move-ins, who had been heavily courted by him at election time, less so. Tempers flared and words were flung—some with measured restraint and some with wild abandon—and for several months, walking into the post office felt like walking into gang territory wearing the wrong colors.

The creation of the monument didn't shift things in a physical way. The land was always federally owned, used by ranchers as pasture and by others as playground, none of which has changed. But it shifted the psychological landscape. It inflamed the land-ownership-by-proximity notion that runs not only through Escalante but through all rural Utah counties and much of the West. It also yielded a not-to-be-missed opportunity for righteous indignation. President Clinton—and for good measure, Bruce Babbitt—were burned in effigy on Main Street in front of Griffin's Grocery.

In the aftermath of the recent flare-up, a pervasive sense of loss and the fear that accompanies it, normally bristling at skin level among longtime residents, hung about town like a heat wave. In Escalante the sorrow of loss is intensified by the single thing we speak about only in small groups if at all: religion. As I stand in front of the single bin of produce displayed in Griffin's Grocery, I hear fears voiced—among those who are not speaking to me—that the town is "dying," that people are leaving to find work elsewhere. In 1950, the population of Escalante was 773; in 2010, it was 797 with a few drops and gains during the six decades in between. The town is not dying, but it is changing. In 2010 only 66 percent of the town's population was Mormon compared with 100 percent in the not-too-distant past—a shift that feels like a slow death to many long-term residents.

When I squeeze by an Escalante local in our tiny post office, the person who grew up in this town, whose mother and grand-mother grew up in this town, it doesn't matter how friendly I am or how good I am or where I came from, I represent her loss. The loss is real, and there's a deep sadness attached to it.

There is a belief among locals that had the monument not been established, the vast and wild (by our modern standards) Kaiparowits Plateau may have been opened to coal mining, establishing jobs for all who wanted them, and those who wanted them would have been the children and the children of children of locals. Utah's senator Orrin Hatch has proclaimed that the monument cost rural Utah "500 high-paying jobs." Whether the Kaiparowits would have become a coal mine is, of course, disputable, and Senator Hatch's lost jobs calculation conveniently unknowable.

But many move-ins share the belief that the establishment of the monument may have prevented the Kaiparowits Plateau from being opened to coal mining. And many are here for exactly that reason—to celebrate and build a life around access to remote space. I'm one of them. Although it took me a while to recognize the grave impact that the loss of space had on me, I know it now and hope to never live without it again.

It is undoubtedly true that the monument has contributed to the religious and ideological shift in Escalante—filled the town with *strangers*, many of them slotted into the catch-all category often heard muttered at the post office with disdain: radical left-wing liberal environmentalist. I proudly hold my position in that category—there's not a single word in that string of words that I'm ashamed to claim. I'm also sixth-generation Mormon and the daughter of a small-time rancher who ran cattle on Utah public lands—arguably the most contentious issue in town—and I proudly hold my position in those categories as well. I have no intent and no means to clean up the contradictions.

The loss of identity to town and people should not be summarily dismissed by those of us causing it. According to geographer Robert Hay, the depth of one's bond to a place is affected by one's ancestral and cultural sense of place. In other words, generations of family on certain land create a deeper spiritual bond to a place than can be created simply by length of residence. That's no small thing, especially to Mormons whose historical story includes the establishment and loss of many beloved towns and places, which is what landed them here 140 years ago.

I moved back to Utah after spending twenty years searching, vowing to never leave again and seeking exactly what Hay mentions—the spiritual bond to my ancestral place. But I found, as many have before me, that my ancestral place is entombed under a Walmart footprint. I understand the sense of loss in Escalante, but I cannot stop it. Nor would I if it meant coal mining the Kaiparowits Plateau, creating in my heart and mind a loss so fathomless there'd be no chance of recovery.

*

The other day, my husband, Steve, and I drove deep into the beautifully sparse and quiet land of the Kaiparowits Plateau— the land of no use. We parked and walked down a wash well traveled by cattle, the prints of which were intermixed with an occasional boot print. Eventually we were enticed into a side canyon that required enough rock-climbing at its entrance to discourage bovine exploration. After we walked for less than an hour in sand free of evidence from man or beast, we reached the steep walls of a box canyon and could go no farther. We spread our lunch and ourselves on a rock and sat in silence, sharing the heat of the sun's rays and listening to birds chatter. Both of us felt it—the dramatic realization that we were alone. Truly alone. We convinced ourselves that no other human had walked that route or lingered on that particular rock in that particular box canyon. Unlikely, but if it is possible anywhere, it is possible on the Kaiparowits Plateau.

I turned to look at Steve. Like a perfectly still lizard, he blends with his environment as if he were given that gift to protect himself from predator—his lanky frame angled to drape effort-lessly over rock, his skin the color of desert sand, his eyes the color of juniper berries. Although he daily lives a life of peace, a palpable tranquility emanated from him at that moment, in that place. I closed my eyes, and felt it also—a reverberating murmur through the body.

There, in the box canyon of the Kaiparowits, I felt deeply something I had only intellectualized before: I knew exactly what we had sacrificed in our zeal to *use* the land. We've sac-rificed the instinctive human, the natural human, the animal human. In doing so, we have sanctioned a painfully slow and ugly death for ourselves. And there's some part of each one of us that knows the truth of this.

I'm not a person who rushes to join many causes, but I have pondered the question, "What matters enough to me to sacrifice what I have?" I found my answer that day on the Kaiparowits Plateau. I would fight the destruction, the tearing apart of this powerful place. There are many arguments for leaving the fossiliferous and geologically rich plateau undisturbed. It can teach, and has taught, us much about our history. But I'm arguing for its protection on a level that cannot be measured in scholarly study, in scientific findings, in dinosaur bones, in dollars, in jobs, or in uses. I'm arguing for something that cannot be measured by any standard generally accepted in our society. I'm arguing for its protection on a spiritual level.

I fear that we are several generations past the human animal now—a fact that some find comforting. I do not. I realize that some who visit the Kaiparowits Plateau and see fine, black silt oozing from the rock will feel nothing more than a sense of wasted opportunity. But left alone, the Kaiparowits Plateau has the capacity to ignite a profound shift in consciousness, has the ability to locate immediate knowledge in the gut. There are few places left in the United States holding on to that sort of potency, and we desperately need them. Let's please, for once in our lives, leave something alone and see if we can't find some human value in that. Let the Kaiparowits Plateau be that one experiment in human restraint, and let's see if we can't recapture a little dignity, a little humility, and maybe even a little humanity in the process.

A DESERT BEYOND FEAR

*Fear is the main source of superstition, and one of
the main sources of cruelty. To conquer fear is the
beginning of wisdom.*

—Bertrand Russell

On a cold, sunny day my husband and I layered up and took ourselves out to our backyard: Grand Staircase-Escalante National Monument. For a few days we had been spiraling downward through a series of miscommunications and tensions—the culmination of my rigorous dedication to fear, or what Bertrand Russell aptly coined "the tyranny of the habit of fear." A fresh storm had dropped ten inches of snow with little moisture, giving the snow an airy, crystallized texture that sprayed out in an arc with each footstep and made a shushing sound, as if it were speaking directly to me. *Shush. Shush. Shush.*

Moving into the elegant world of white-draped red rock is usually enough to strip our minds of the qualms that harass us, but on this day, Steve and I both stomped into the desert bearing a commitment to hang on to the somber roles we had adopted. Solemnity is difficult, however, when one is tumbling down hills of snow-covered deep sand and skidding off steep angles of slickrock on one's backside. Still, it took a good half mile before we were convinced of our absurdity.

Such is the nature of the desert. If you persist in your gravity, the desert will take full advantage. It will have you falling over yourself as you trudge along carrying your blame and angst and fear. It will mock you until you literally and figuratively lighten up and conform to the place. The place will never conform to you. We knew that; that's why we went. That's why we always go to the desert when we're stuck in a cycle of self-induced wretchedness.

I learned fear early and I learned it well. I had two good role models. My father was fearful of not being adored by all. That fear determined his every action and his every thought. If proper adoration was not forthcoming, his temper flared. He provided me with my first experience—and many follow-ups—of fear. He taught me that danger is ever-present and unpredictable and that hypervigilance is a good approach—maybe the only sane approach—to life.

My mother, a sweet and tender woman, was fearful of life in general. If at any given time I didn't exhibit enough fear, she feared for me, quietly but persistently expressing her worries and words of caution. My mother carried a "wound of catastrophic expectations," as termed by psychotherapist Dick Olney, acquired the summer of her thirteenth year when her father was killed in an accident. From that point forward, my mother anticipated the worst from life—as did her own mother—and spent much of her life seeking safe haven. Indeed, that may have been an unconscious singular goal of hers: safety. She spoke of the accident with a sadness that seemed to acknowledge her entrapment in the "tyranny of the habit of fear." As she aged, her definition of safe haven changed to fit her circumstances, so that in the end, I believe, she died having found it. Lifetime goal achieved. It took me beyond half a century to realize I had sub-consciously adopted my mother's goal.

Safety sires caution. Caution breeds fear.

The list of things I've feared at some point in my life is long: dogs, my father, cockroaches, a lack of friends, a lack of solitude, horses, cows, being yelled at, being ignored, love, sex, the lack of love and sex, being alone, being in a relationship, going to school, missing school, being hungry, being poor, being stupid, being stranded in the middle of an ocean (although I never go into the middle of oceans), financial destitution, aging, illness, darkness, parties, being wrong, being hated, being criticized, dressing inappropriately for any occasion, not fitting in, con-forming, backpacking alone, backpacking in groups, drugs, lack of drugs, heartbreak, humiliation, having nothing to say, saying too much, and, of course, fear itself. The list is endless and cumbersome to navigate.

"Fear," Russell writes, "makes man unwise in the three great departments of human conduct: his dealings with nature, his dealings with other men, and his dealings with himself."

That sums it up pretty well. I've spent many lifetime hours processing fear, and I've brought fear's oppression into my mar-riage. Because fear is my natural state of mind, I often don't realize I'm spewing it into the world with my words and actions. The incident that drove us into the desert on that particular day was, in my mind, a simple expression of concern, a few "what will happen ifs"; in Steve's mind, a paranoid rant. Upon reflec-tion, I have to agree with his version.

A few months prior, Steve and I had decided upon a change in our lives: We traded certainty, in the form of a bi-weekly paycheck, for joy, in the form of writing time. It wasn't a rash decision; it was a decision five years in the making. Yet from the moment the last check was cashed, my fear began roiling, slowly at first, but soon popping and splashing out of its shallow container. My voiced concerns regarding insolvency and homelessness were considerably beyond probable, falling to the far side of remotely possible. In my world, that's enough for worry, discussion, obsession, more discussion, and many consecutive nights of insomnia.

We had parked the truck at the "head of the rocks," an understated description of a spot that allows a 360-degree view of Grand Staircase-Escalante National Monument's vast expanse of red and white slickrock cut with deep gulches and painted with the sweeping wear of wind and water. Before we moved to the small town of Escalante on the monument's border, we would come here from our city home five hours away—alone or together—whenever life threatened to shut us down.

From the head of the rocks, we followed the old cream cellar road, a wagon trail of switchbacks carved into stone in the early 1900s. We could see our destination about two miles out, a smooth, jutting wall with a level run of sand at its base that would allow us to sit with our faces to the sun and our backs against the wall. A fitting spot.

Steve walked behind me in silence, but I knew his thoughts. My fear perplexes and disparages him. His acts of heroism should dispel my anxiety, but it persists beyond the reach of his love. Yet, his love, too, persists.

Knowing I'll pick up and read anything placed in my path, Steve had left on the butcher block where I eat breakfast Russell's timeless collection of essays *New Hopes for a Changing World,* published in 1951. I skimmed the table of contents until I reached three essays entitled, "Fear," "Fortitude," and "Life without Fear," in which Russell writes about the pervasive and destructive nature of fear. One of the significant fears Russell writes about—a fear apparently close to his own heart—is the fear of being unlovable, which, he writes, is self-fulfilling unless one gets out from under fear's dominion. I've been testing Russell's theory for thirteen years now.

I've heard it said that all fear stems from the knowledge of our own mortality, and indeed, many of our social systems thrive by exploiting our fear of death and our desire to thwart it. But fear of death has never been my problem. Life, not death, holds the promise of misery. Maybe this position is not so strange for someone who has habitually viewed life as a minefield to be navigated. When life is lived as a problem to be solved, death offers the ultimate resolution, the release of all fears, the moment of pure peace.

By the time we had dropped from the head of the rocks halfway down to the scooped-out basin below, I could feel Steve letting go. His stride had become rhythmic, his foot placement sure. Steve's six-foot-four lanky frame flows effortlessly through the desert. He's a native species. If I turned to look at him, I would see a serene expression on his face, his hands held in front of his chest, the fingertips gently touching—his walking contemplation pose. When we reached our destination, Steve pulled a space blanket from his pack and spread it for us to sit on. The warm rock allowed us to discard several layers of clothing before resting our backs on the wall and tipping our faces upward. Steve placed a hand on my leg.

In his autobiography, Russell writes, "In general, I find that things that have happened to me out-of-doors have made a deeper impression than things that have happened indoors." A curious statement upon first read, but my desert rambles have confirmed that nothing illuminates irrational fear more brilliantly than sun bouncing off slickrock.

"My fear is a bit much," I said.

"Yes," Steve replied.

"The tyranny of the habit of fear."

Sometimes in the morning I wake up feeling as if my world is about to fly apart, and it takes a few minutes to pull myself back into my bed, my bedroom, my house—the one where my kind and loving husband moves around the kitchen making coffee, the one where a sweet, asthmatic cat has taken up the still-warm, vacated space on the bed next to me.

I once had a therapist tell me that I likely learned my fear at a preverbal stage of life, which means, as I understand it, it got hardwired in my brain. She called it Armageddon Syndrome. A good, descriptive assessment. It is the deep nature of my fear that makes it an all-or-nothing proposition for me, something that needs to be treated like an addiction. Dabbling in it, however briefly, is sure to bring on a full-scale blackout. The only option is letting go entirely—one moment at a time. Such is my goal: a steady practice of letting go of fear until I find myself at peace. For someone like me, that's no small journey. It's akin to a longtime drug user—living among many other drug users—trying to get clean. From that place of peace, however transient it may be, I plan to live until I die.

I've had throughout my life what I refer to as moments of bravado, a sudden urge to push myself beyond my fear in some big way. Those are the moments responsible for the significant changes in my life. They took me from my hometown of Tooele, Utah, to New York City, from accounting to writing, and from New York City back home to the West where I belong. Ultimately, my moments of bravado took me to the deserts of the Escalante, a place so stunning in its grandeur it defies fear. If ever there were a place on earth that allows one to enter and dwell at peace, this would be it.

From the outside looking in, my moments of bravado may appear as a connected life—a life lived with courage and intent. Yet each moment was taken in sheer terror. In *The Courage to Create,* Rollo May writes that Kierkegaard, Nietzsche, Camus, and Sartre all defined courage not as the absence of fear, but as the ability to act in spite of fear. A life of courage can be lived in small ways, through small decisions. If I go by that definition, I can technically call myself courageous.

Treating my fear as an addiction that doesn't allow wavering often means placing myself in what others see as risky situations: I quit well-paying jobs to write full time; I leave "safe" relationships in search of love and passion; I flee to the red rock to hike when I'm supposed to be earning money; I push out into the deserts of the Colorado Plateau each spring, unprepared and out of shape, with a thirty-five-pound pack strapped to my back. Many consider my actions foolish, and I often believe the same myself. How wise is it for a woman who fears financial destitution to quit her job (the one with a good salary and health insurance!) during the worst economy on recent record?

The answer lies in Russell's words: "Until you have admitted your own fears to yourself, and have guarded yourself by a difficult effort of will against their mythmaking power, you cannot hope to think truly about many matters of great importance."

Fear is noisy, and it takes up a lot of space. Very little else—including matters of great importance—can break through. But every once in a while, if I sit on my porch and quiet myself long enough to hear the birds pecking at the fallen walnuts under the black walnut tree, in the part of my gut that is often churning with anxiety, I know that all of the "risky" decisions I've identified above are the only things that *do* keep my world from flying apart.

When I wake up in the swirl of Armageddon, I have two choices. The first is to lie in bed convincing myself, which takes no more than ten seconds, that the headlines are looming nearby—I will soon lose my house, my husband, and what little money I have. I can probably keep the cat, but he and I will be sharing a food bowl. The other choice is the courageous choice: get out of bed, open the blinds, and look to the east where the Escalante River gorge cuts through the sunlit ridge.

STAY

*Home is like religion. Sensibly you understand the
need for it, yet not even sensible people can explain it.*

—Ellen Meloy

I have not traveled much. In my demographic—middle-age, middle-class, educated liberal—my nomadic shortcomings are seen as piteous, bordering on disgraceful. I've heard the refrain used to explain the full range of human failings: *She's never been anywhere!* At the root of most problems, apparently, lies travel negligence—as if stepping *on* a plane in Cincinnati and *off* in Bombay immediately transforms one from a nitwit into Gandhi.

Upon discovery of my travel vacuity, an acquaintance once told me that she considered travel an essential part of educating her children, thereby implicating not only my dereliction but also that of my parents. I nodded my approval while she rattled off names of distant places that had, through the years, transformed her children from ignoramuses into perceptive young adults. I could find no point upon which to disagree, but a twinge of defensiveness edged along my spine.

When I was seven, my family took a car trip from our rural Utah home to the Grand Canyon in the middle of July—a thousand miles with a kid hanging out every window to ward off heat prostration. Another year, we did Yellowstone Park in much the same manner. That was the extent of my parents' education-through-travel curriculum.

Upon moving first to Salt Lake City and later to New York City, I learned that low mileage is not valued in humans as it is in automobiles. Still, back in the day when photos were kept where they belong—in a cardboard box stuffed in the back of an overburdened closet until a family death demands transference—one could circumvent the conversation. Now, photographic proof of travel—clearly as essential as the travel itself—is portable. It can be (and is) in your face instantly and often.

A while back, an essay in the *New York Times* by inveterate traveler Paul Theroux caught my attention with this statement: "'Don't go there,' the know-it-all, stay-at-home finger wagger says of many a distant place. I have heard it my whole traveling life, and in almost every case it was bad advice." I don't know in what sort of social circles Theroux moves, but I've never met a stay-at-homer who had a fighting chance in a finger-wagging match with a swaggering globetrotter.

Filled with righteous indignation, I mentioned Theroux's reproach to my husband who astutely replied, "The fewer topics we insist on turning into moral issues, the better." Such a philosophy can ease many of life's annoyances, but in this case I'm compelled to take a moral stand. I speak for nonvoyagers shrinking in corners of cocktail parties and ducking words lobbed in their direction—*Have you been? Oh, you haven't? But you must!*—while nearby the host flaunts the Donggang Boat Burning Festival as her entry into the unofficial and omnipresent best travel story contest, and two other guests jovially compete for worst taxi ride with Mexico City and Moscow.

I often choose that precise moment to shift the conversation to the next most popular topic at such parties—buying local, eating local, living local—which most can speak about with equal aplomb and nary a note of conflict. Even on that particular topic there remains a note of superiority in the voices of the well traveled, as if one can appreciate living locally only if one has been endowed with the sensibilities derived from traveling extensively. An editor at an esteemed eastern newspaper recently wrote to say, "I'm not sure the idea of living locally and... travel are really at odds," and the only response I could rouse was, "I'm not sure why you're not sure." What part of the living-locally doctrine condones continent hopping on transatlantic flights?

Air travel spreads disease, consumes massive amounts of fossil fuels, leaves sun-blocking pollution in otherwise clear skies, and spews greenhouse gasses into the atmosphere at levels that, according to a 2010 MIT study, kill an estimated ten thousand people a year. Yet we hop on airplanes with full confidence in the merit of our actions.

I haven't always been so disagreeable on the issue of travel. My first inclination when chided for my behavior is to assume that there are right ways to live a life and wrong ways to live a life, and I'm probably doing it wrong. I grew up in a small, blue-collar town sheltered by a dominant religion. I didn't manage to find my way to college until my late twenties, and then didn't manage to follow up with graduate school until my forties. By all generally accepted standards of measuring a good life, I need guidance. So, as directed, I've taken a trip or two to *broaden my horizons.*

Most recently, my husband and I took the quintessential Roman holiday; I was Audrey Hepburn and he was Gregory Peck. We walked rainy cobblestone streets, soaked up art and architecture and history, spent a day with the Catholics, and gorged on great food. And we enjoyed every minute of it. Did I pick up a little knowledge, a little culture? Certainly. Am I a *better* person for having "done" Rome? Probably not. Nor did I arrive home ready to join the masses in unfettered celebration of the goodness of travel.

When questioned about my lack of mileage accumulation, I resort to a short, conversation-ending lie: I can't afford to travel. (That will not work, by the way, with your proud budget-traveler who will whip out a smartphone, pull up Airbnb.com, and hand you a thirty-day European itinerary to fit even the smallest budget.) The truth is that I'm not interested in competitions that tally up continents and countries and colorful passport stamps. I care nothing about producing a long list (and photos!) of the places I've touched down upon the earth. I want to be able to *feel* a place. So that what begins as me entering the place transforms—in turn and in time—into the place entering me. I want to experience the slight shift in consciousness and the small opening of the heart that almost any place can offer if we pause long enough to allow it.

According to National Park Service surveys, the average time a visitor spends experiencing the Grand Canyon—the 1-mile-deep and 277-mile-long magnificent gash in the earth—is seventeen minutes. Seen. Done. At Lower Calf Creek Trailhead in Grand Staircase-Escalante National Monument—often found on the same itinerary as the Grand Canyon—visitors check watches and cell phones and run time/distance calculations in their heads. They can make it to Lower Calf Creek Falls, snap the iconic photo—a waterfall in the desert—and be slithering through the lustrous pink walls of a slot canyon by afternoon. Once they have dispatched one or both of those things, the monument can be checked off. Three more nearby national

parks await, so square the place up through a lens; you can
see it later on a computer screen. Those seven-hundred-year-
old pictographs? Imagine how great they will look magnified,
cropped, and photoshopped.

People chatter and scurry along Calf Creek Trail and puff with
pride when passing dawdlers like me. Having reached the falls
and started back, they excitedly report the presumed destination ETA—*Almost there! Thirty more minutes!*—never doubting
that speed and efficiency are universal human values.

Grand Staircase-Escalante National Monument is my place.
I live here. I avoid Calf Creek during the busiest and noisiest
months, but the trail goes dormant in winter. In the silence and
solitude of those frigid days, I am lured off trails, into side canyons, and over boulders to the highest smooth canyon walls.
There, I sit in the sand, face to the sun, back against the rock
upon which an ancient painted figure—boxy and black with red
arms—hovers above my head. He is surrounded by painted and
etched hands and joined by two more red figures on a nearby
wall. From my perch I can see, on a high ledge across the canyon,
a granary in immaculate condition, impossibly inaccessible to
the clumsy people we have become.

Few visitors have been here. It's not marked on any map
or noted in any guidebook. It is found by happenstance, by
aimless wandering, by frittering away time. In much the same
manner, my husband and I once happened upon a relatively
untouched domicile and found seven-hundred-year-old corncobs lying in the dirt. That's my education through travel. It
was the first time I fully understood the enormous impact of
the garbage I'll leave behind on the earth. Archeologists are
thrilled by what the corncobs tell them about the Fremont
Indians, the canyon's former occupants, but I'm thinking future

humans—if there are any—will be less thrilled by what trails behind me.

If I settle myself into stillness, breathe slowly and deeply, I can *feel* the lives lived in this place. A deep truth resonates here, an inner rumbling that links the story of every human to the next human and every species to every other species, but we're moving too quickly and buzzing too loudly to get it.

To those who would accuse me of romanticizing place and people, I would ask only that you sit still and quiet in this place—or your own place—for an extended period. The wonder of a place is its indifference to us—to our pain, our fear, our prerequisites. Such indifference is a gift, a teacher. Without it, we consider ourselves the center of the universe, a conviction that is proving embarrassingly wide of the mark.

W. H. Auden said, "We are lived by the powers we pretend to understand." Sitting still in a place like this is as close as I, up against the limitations of my human mind, will ever get to understanding the powers that live me.

We have sacrificed something crucial in the last seven hundred years. As modern humans, we've chosen compartmentalization over fullness, the pieces over the whole. We've broken life into parts, placed the mind in the brain, separated brain from body, pulled apart body and soul, and ripped ourselves away from nature to occupy the throne of dominion.

Many of us live with a sense of unrest as we try to understand and assemble our disparate parts, as we attempt to puzzle them back into a whole life. We travel to gather bits of experience that are supposed to make us *more* or *better* than we currently are, and we seek spirituality as a consumer product. We enthusiastically sign up for the Buddha Circuit Tour and jet off to view the place Buddha sat in stillness for a full forty-nine days. Sitting under a panel of rock art, I find good reason to appreciate the whole lives of those who sat here before me. I doubt they yearned to conquer five continents, let alone other planets. I question whether yearning was part of their lives at all.

I have often wondered if *staying* for me is a circumstance of fate. Had I been blessed with financial means would I be one of the widely traveled sharing stories at cocktail parties? I suspect not. An indefinable combination of life's offerings and deficits brought me here, and I want to know why my homing device is set to the coordinates of dark sandstone canyons. My knowledge of this place is the depth of a rain puddle, yet somehow I know that my understanding of this place is fundamental to my understanding of this life. Both of those things may be out of my reach, but the pursuit seems worthy nonetheless.

I want the wisdom this place offers—not to make me more knowledgeable but to make me whole, to fill the gaps in my being. On my darkest days, the days when my anxiety surges, the days when I believe the message of my modern brain: *a full bank account is the path to peace*—on those days I travel. Not to Myanmar, not to Tanzania, but to this place—a spot in the sand below a black shaman with red arms—because this is where my modern brain is quieted by my ancient soul. And it whispers *stay, listen.*

ON WALKING

*All the efforts to control who strolls and how suggest
that walking may in some way still be subversive...
it provides entertainment in which nothing is spent
or consumed.*

—Rebecca Solnit

Childhood Walks

I became a lustful wanderer at a young age. No cars idled outside
my elementary school at day's end to gather children, a legacy
of time and place. When the bell rang, kids shot through every
exit and scattered in all directions under their own might. What
is now considered a high-risk parenting deficiency—losing track
of your kid—was then an immense gift. Each twenty-minute
walk from school to home became a ninety-minute adventure.

From kindergarten through fourth grade, my route home
took me through a field and along a ditch bank, and if I didn't
mind wading the ditch and climbing a chain link fence into
my backyard, I never had to step foot on a sidewalk. On my
daily walk I learned about rocks and bugs and horny toads
and grasses. I learned to love mud and the crispy edges of ice.
I learned that I'm a toucher. Trees, fences, plants, walls—anything nearby—I impulsively reach for them and that's why all
my gloves have holes in the fingertips. To this day, I covet the

sense of touch, oft forgotten sibling of sight, sound, taste, and smell. If I can scoop up a bit of the surface beneath my feet—dirt, mud, or sand—to tickle the soft center of my palm as I walk, I am filled with silly joy.

On those early walks I practiced swearing and lying and became quite good at both. I practiced throwing—rocks, snowballs, and dirt clods—but never became good at it. I learned that I like walking with a single friend, but I dislike walking in groups. I learned that I'm destined to be going the opposite direction of friends. I learned to love solitude.

Through those walks I came to see that the outside world is beautiful, rich, and peaceful, and the inside world is considerably less so. In most instances, the outside world is the safer of the two.

Daily Walks

From my front door, the loop around the circumference of my town is 3.4 miles. During the hour it takes me to walk the loop, I am not tracked by Internet clicks; I am not reachable by e-mail or phone; I am, in fact, barely noticed. It is the happiest hour of my day.

Historic Walks

Seven of my eight great-great-grandmothers walked all or part of the Mormon Trail. I have not researched the travels of my great-great-grandfathers, but I suppose many of them did also. Great-Great-Grandmother Anna Maria walked the trail pregnant, then gave birth to a stillborn baby. Great-Great-Grandmother Hannah, a member of the doomed Martin Handcart Company, would leave her dead son's body along the trail in a shallow grave near the North Platte River. She and her two young daughters would survive, although Hannah's feet were so damaged it would be a year after getting to Utah before she would take another step.

I've often wondered if I'm genetically predisposed to walking—more so than the average person—but I've seen little evidence of it in my lifetime. My mother walked only at my side, and I don't remember my grandmothers as walkers. In my small town—made up mostly of descendants from lineage similar to my own—walking is an anomaly. The post office sits within three blocks of almost every house in town, yet the parking lot is always full of idling sedans and pickup trucks. It's as if the Mormons sat down to rest after walking the trail and never got up again. A twelve-hundred-mile walk requires a long rest—maybe two hundred years.

Natural Walks

On a spring day, cool with sharp sunshine, my husband, Steve, and I walked into the slickrock of Strike Valley Overlook at the entrance to Upper Muley Twist near Boulder, Utah, and found a notch in the rocks out of the breeze. When I pulled off boots and socks, heat-storing slickrock sent warmth up my body through the soles of my feet. Enticed to place more skin against warm rocks, every article of clothing was soon cast aside. Steve did the same. Then he held out his hand and said, "Walk with me."

"Really?" I asked.

"Sure," he said.

"What if we see someone?"

He shrugged.

Barefoot across slickrock, we left our clothing behind and walked for an hour. Within minutes, what felt initially uncomfortable became natural, honest. Steve had been walking naked in slickrock deserts for more than 30 years when I met him, an act driven not by prurience but by nature. His connection to the natural world had never been severed, the organic feral part of him retained and nurtured. With those three words—walk with me—he began the restoration of mine.

Inefficient Walks

I once boasted to Steve that I had never reached my walking capacity, that although I might grow weary, my legs would keep moving across the landscape regardless of my mental or physical state. I believe he took that as a challenge.

My boast came to be tested on the last day of a stunningly beautiful fifty-mile walk through Paria Canyon in the Arizona Strip on my forty-ninth birthday. The first day's travel through fourteen miles of a deep, narrow slot called Buckskin Gulch was more obstacle course than walk. It required slogging through ice-cold, waist-high, stagnant pools with packs held overhead, bellying under logjams dragging packs behind on a rope, and a final rappel down a short, vertical drop.

We reached the confluence with Paria River at dusk, bedraggled and happy. As we walked a gauntlet past already-settled campers watching us with a mixture of curiosity, superiority, and pity (maybe even suspicion—dueling banjos played in my exhausted mind), I expressed my bewilderment. Only three other hikers had shuttled to the trailhead with us, and the permits granted to hike the full fifty miles were limited. Steve explained that most campers had arrived via a seven-mile shortcut to the confluence and would be leaving the same way. Efficient hikers, poor souls. Let them smugly sip their cocktails while we set up camp on a narrow sandbar in the falling darkness, for only we knew what they had missed: fourteen miles of travel between red sandstone walls that gently brush your body as you pass.

One of the most sensual walks a human can take through the earth: seductive, erotic, ravishing.

In his 1968 Pulitzer Prize–winning book *So Human an Animal*, Rene Dubos predicted that spending most of our days among "concrete and steel... in the midst of noise, dirt, ugliness, and absurdity" threatened our very "humanness." I would argue that the world since 1968 has become noisier and significantly more absurd, and the need to remove ourselves from that world, more essential. Yet when we have opportunity to do so, we take the shortcut.

At one time, the most coveted destination in the Escalante Canyons was somewhat protected by a seven-mile walk through deep sand, so that when you arrived and leaned your tired body against a Navajo sandstone wall soaring several hundred feet above you, when you gently dipped your aching feet into the clear creek, your soul opened naturally and filled with gratitude. Every clumsy step taken had value. Then some clever person created a shortcut off a rock face, thereby opening the destination to a two-mile walk. You can now drop in, snap your photos, and get back to the concrete and steel world before sundown. What risk to our humanness, I wonder, is the loss of twelve thousand slow and deliberate steps?

In her book *Wanderlust: The History of Walking*, Rebecca Solnit writes, "Walking... is how the body measures itself against the earth." But I found that if you walk long enough under the right circumstances, the body stops pushing *against* the earth and begins to blend *with* the earth in rhythm and tone. On our fifty-mile walk through Paria Canyon, our bodies attracted the elements as if they had gone through years of deprivation; it felt right to be water-doused, sunbaked, sand-exfoliated, and wind-brushed. We stopped to gape at twenty-foot hanging gardens; we paused to drink from natural fountains flowing forth from cracks in the walls; we swam under waterfalls and bathed in clear, deep pools. So inefficient was our walk that on the last day, the day our permits expired, we still had eleven miles to go.

I assumed we were simply going to walk down the Paria River until it dumped us into the Colorado River at Lee's Ferry, which is technically correct. Eleven miles is, for me, a full day with a heavy pack but not impossible. But unlike the miles that came before, a leisurely stroll since leaving Buckskin Gulch, the last eleven required many overland detours to navigate substantial drops in elevation. Every so often, the river narrowed, dropped over the edge of a rock cliff, pooled for a moment at the bottom, and went merrily on its way.

Standing at the top of those falls never failed to remind me that we are one of the most inadequate and awkward animals walking the earth. Solnit describes the human body as a "column of flesh and bone, always in danger of toppling...the upright body's various sections balanced on top of each other...a proud, unsteady tower" whereas "four-legged animals are as steady as a table." And, I might add, considerably more nimble.

With the drop in elevation came a rise in temperature to 110 degrees, a notable absence of even a sliver of shade, and a trail of deep sand that worked its way into socks leaving skin rubbed raw and leading to a significant slowdown in my pace.

Because Steve and I have walked together for many years, an unspoken system has developed between us. When one exhausted person finds a walking rhythm—a zone—the other exhausted person doesn't interrupt it. Our hiking style, when one of us has a rhythm and the other has slowed to a crawl, is a fine balance between ditching a person entirely and knowing when to stop, wait, or retrace steps.

I had lost sight of Steve about ten minutes before I reached the cutoff that would take me from the riverbed to Lee's Ferry Landing, which meant the truck was less than a mile away. The sun was blessedly dropping low in the sky, and a short crawl up a three-foot sandy embankment presented the only obstacle between me and the concrete world. After three attempts, the bank breaking away under my feet each time, I knew I was in trouble. I tried two more times. Then I dumped my pack, dropped to the ground, and began casting about for the efficient shortcut while I waited for Steve to find me.

City Walks

Since moving to a small town, I miss city walking. I miss the strangeness of humans, what they create, what they leave behind. In the desert, I'd prefer not to see another human or human remnant less than seven hundred years old. But in a city, I value the opposite. I want to walk among people and their detritus, able to stare and study with anonymity.

The city I know best, Salt Lake City, is built on a Mormon grid so one can never get lost. That might be my favorite bequest from my Mormon ancestors. Once you know the starting point—the southeast cornerstone of the Mormon temple grounds—you can navigate to any Salt Lake City address without aid of map or GPS. Visitors often find this system confusing and frustrating, but given enough time, one is forced to admit its brilliance.

In the older parts of town, the grid allowed large lots, wide streets, and big square blocks split in half with a narrow alley that runs between the backyards of houses facing opposite directions. Walking the back alleys is the outside equivalent of snooping through a medicine cabinet. I have peeked through wooden slats and passed slowly to eavesdrop on conversations conducted under a false sense of confidentiality.

A few years ago, a fashion trend dictated that the folks on Salt Lake City's east side—the trendsetting side—leave many of their windows curtainless. Assuming people could choose privacy over fashion if so desired, I gawked shamelessly. I witnessed happy dinners, sad dinners, loud dinners, lonely dinners. I saw lives filled with television, books, laughter, tears, embraces, friends, and solitude. Mostly television.

Shortly after we married, Steve and I used to leave our house in the Ninth and Ninth area of Salt Lake City around 10:00 p.m. each Friday and walk into the early hours of the morning. We did this in every season, in every kind of weather, exploring each other while we explored our city. Conversations that feel invasive and insidious in the confines of four walls flow effortlessly while walking, as if the literal pumping of blood required to move the body coincides with a metaphorical opening of the heart.

On airless summer nights we'd loiter on park benches and make out like teenagers. On winter nights, among steady, fat flakes of snow, we'd drop off the city streets into Bonneville Glen where a dirt trail runs along Red Butte Creek. Shrouded in snowy limbs and silenced by snow, the place hovered between pristine beauty and eerie isolation, an immeasurable offering for anyone willing to move on two feet.

We've walked gardens, industrial warehouses, junkyards, quaint neighborhoods, wealthy neighborhoods, poor neighborhoods, urban streets, creek banks, parks, and cemeteries. We've ducked into open houses pretending to be buyers, walked through office buildings and hospitals looking for unlocked bathrooms, and sat in churches to rest.

We know the beauty of the city, and we know its ugliness. We know the parts that flower and die, the parts that change, the parts that disappear, and the parts that hang on year after year. And through walking, we know each other the same way.

Purposeful Walks

In spring 2009, shortly after moving to Escalante, I had what a doctor called "a series of unfortunate events" that included the extraction of a fractured tooth, antibiotics, an infected cyst, more antibiotics, and an allergic reaction to antibiotics, all of which triggered a twelve-week bout of shingles. Shingles pain is breath-stealing severe. Medications and lidocaine patches barely took the edge off, and within thirty minutes—five and a half hours before the next dose—the pain was back full bore. In the worst of it, I would look at Steve to see a face twisted and drained of color as if he were the one experiencing it. He later confessed that watching me grapple with the pain of shingles reminded him of watching his brother die from cancer. One day Steve suggested that walking in the desert might make me feel better. I thought him crazy, and to prove it, I agreed to go.

I curled into the passenger seat of the truck during the ten-minute drive out of town, wrapped tightly in my own arms to mitigate the agony of every bump and jolt. When he pulled off the road, I jumped out and started walking before he brought the truck to a full stop. He would have to catch up; I had pain to outrun.

I bushwhacked cross-country and dropped into a small wash that eventually leads to Phipps Wash and Phipps Arch. Turned out Steve was right. As long as I was moving, the pain was tolerable. When I stopped, the pain caught up with me. We walked that day until dusk forced us home.

During the following three months, Phipps Wash became hallowed territory. I went every day, sometimes all day, to walk off pain. Although Phipps Arch is a popular hike, I never saw another person, never had to explain the grimace on my face or my need to keep moving. I could—and did—howl and cry at will. Phipps is where I walk now when life becomes difficult, noisy, confusing. It seems many types of pain can be outwalked. When Steve and I get tangled in each other's nets, he knows where to find me.

Salty Walks

On the lonely north shore of the Great Salt Lake when the lake is low, you can walk for miles across a slab of salt that covers the sand like ice. I recommend it.

Undesirable Walks

Treadmills and shopping malls.

Mother Walks

One weekend, my mother and I took the train from Williams, Arizona, to the Grand Canyon. The train trip was anticlimactic—one of those goofy Wild West operations with mock train robberies and such—but we had a full weekend ahead of us. I knew she wouldn't be able to hike—her body contained the twists and torment of rheumatoid arthritis—but miles of easy strolling along the rim trail awaited us. After we settled into Maswik Lodge, a ten-minute walk from the rim, we entered the warm evening to go to dinner. We had walked less than twenty yards when she dropped onto the nearest bench. Tears flowed freely down her face. Alarmed, I sat beside her and waited for an explanation.

"I can't do it," she said. "I can't make it to dinner. I can't walk that far."

"Huh?" I said. "What do you mean you can't walk? You mean you can't walk?"

That's what she meant. At some point, while my attention was turned toward my own life, she had lost her ability to walk more than a few steps. She was crying, I knew, not for the loss of her own mobility but for the moment she disappointed her daughter. Walking had been our way of moving through the world together. We had walked the hills and beaches around small Mexican villages; we had walked New York City and San Francisco; we had walked the streets of Tucson where I lived and the streets of Tooele where she lived. And we had walked the streets of Salt Lake City for almost five decades. I mourned the loss of her arm in mine—as she knew I would—maybe more than I mourned her death five years later.

After she died, I spent a crazy number of hours walking Salt Lake City alone, noting the places she would have loved—a hidden set of narrow crumbling stairs, an overgrown and for-gotten cemetery. I always walked—and still do whenever I have the chance—through her beloved Mormon temple grounds, a place that filled her with pride for the religion she lived and cherished. Toward her last days, I pushed her through the lush temple gardens in a wheelchair, an attempt to keep the two of us in motion. I would push her wheelchair to the edge of a garden box filled with purple and pink pansies, sit on the speckled granite ledge, and take her crippled hands in mine.

"Your hands are beginning to look like mine," she once said. "Do they hurt?"

"No," I lied, not wanting her to know and not willing to admit to myself that I, too, may reach a day when I can no longer walk.

THE CURLING FINGERS
OF THE HATCH WOMEN

I believe in women.

—Emmeline B. Wells

Shortly after my forty-eighth birthday I moved home to Utah. I had been gone more than twenty years, some of it in New York City, most of it in Tucson. I returned to pursue love with the man who is now my husband, and I returned to be with my mother at the end of her life. But mostly I returned because I spent my childhood in the shadow of the Oquirrhs, because I became an adult in the shadow of the Wasatch, and because those mountains hold the knowledge of the person I was, the person I could have been, and the person I am. I always knew I would return.

One spring day, a few years before my mother died, I sat at the kitchen table in my childhood home in Tooele, Utah, and skimmed a newspaper while my mother prepared a lesson she was to give in church on Sunday. As her left hand brushed over the pages of a Book of Mormon, only the tips of her fingers and the base of her wrist made contact with the delicate paper; she was unable to rest her hand flat upon the page. Her right hand curled around a pen, and she slowly and painfully made notes, rings glittering incongruously on the bent claw. Now, almost ten years after her death, I still remember the feel of her curled hand in mine—loose skin, protruding veins, twisted knuckles.

Under the pretense of comforting her, I used to stroke her hand, seeking solace for myself.

I noticed the curled hands of the Hatch women—my mother and her three sisters—as if they were spring-loaded and tripped overnight, first Agatha, followed in age order by Carrell, Leona, and my mother, Darlene. All four women had the curling fingers of my grandmother, Ethel Hatch. The Hatch women blamed the Gooch women—my grandmother's sisters and her mother— but it is a Hatch trait now and I will unfortunately but proudly carry it forward. Shortly before I turned forty, when I started to feel pain at the base of my thumbs, I began to ask about the hands. My mother and aunts shrugged, as if I were asking why the sun rises or why the seasons change.

Every morning now my hands scrabble with containers of calcium tablets, fish oil softgels, glucosamine chondroitin capsules, and a host of antioxidant vitamins before I lackadaisically pop them in my mouth. I put no faith in the pills, the gluten-free diet, the walking regime, the yoga, the bioidentical hormone-replacement therapy, green tea, or a multitude of herbs I've tried in the past twenty years while the pain in my hands has intensified. They are Hatch hands, now curled, as if they hold a fond memory of gripping a Ball fruit jar filled with pear halves.

I never saw my grandmother's hands before they began to curl. They fascinated me, all the things they could do in that condition. I saw them black with dirt from digging potatoes, I saw them red and raw from scrubbing pots, and later, I saw them resigned and lifeless, hanging over the arms of a wheelchair, jeweled with a single gold band, but I never saw them straight and strong.

At the Sunshine Terrace rest home in Logan, Utah, where my grandmother spent her final days, she would ask to be wheeled to the patio to sit among birds and honeysuckle, the sickly sweet smell of which would call forth memories. Mom and I sat on either side of her, a hand placed lightly on one of her knotted claws as they rested on the chair's cold steel. One side of my grandmother's face was paralyzed, blinded, and deafened by the accident that took her husband when she was forty-four, and whenever she got ready to tell a story, she would twist her head and fix her good eye on me, offer up her sad half smile, and speak in the cheerless voice of an old woman who had finished life long before her body would acknowledge it. A certain part of those stories remains uncomfortably lodged in me—as was her intent—like a piece of rotting wood in the sludge of a drying riverbed: the unbroken chain of never-idle hands in service to God and the Mormon Church.

My great-great-grandmother Anna Maria Larsen was twenty-nine years old and pregnant when she placed her young hands on the splintering holds of a handcart piled high with food, cooking utensils, and bedding. Encountering rain, wind, dust, and insects, she and her husband, Hans, averaged fifteen miles a day pulling the cart thirteen hundred miles along the Mormon Trail from Iowa City to Salt Lake City. Anna Maria settled in Brigham City and gave birth to eight children, five of whom died as infants. "Needed by God" is the notation next to their names in the family history. She began a lifelong work of sewing men's suits and women's dresses, her young daughter Mary Ann by her side, threading needles for her mother with nimble fingers.

Years later, Mary Ann Gooch, my great-grandmother, put her mother's teaching to use sewing burial clothes. In her capacity as a Relief Society member of the Mormon Church in Rich, Idaho, she embraced her assigned duties to wash and dress the dead before they entered the ground, ascended to heaven, and met with God.

In the only photograph I have of her, Mary Ann Gooch looks straight out at me. She is a stalwart woman, much more so than her daughter, my grandmother. As I look at the photo, I place a finger over the softball-sized goiter protruding below her right ear, above her collar. The face is solemn but not unpleasant. When I remove my finger, the face becomes stern, almost frightening. There are worse things to inherit than aching hands.

My grandmother's own life followed the pattern sewn by her mother and grandmother: a life of service to others. She raised eight children, her youngest, my mother, only thirteen when she lost her husband. She cooked meals and washed dishes at the Sigma Chi fraternity house at Utah State University, and she took care of old women in their homes until she needed the same herself.

Grandmother ended each story she told with a firm caution: the devil and idle hands work together. Then she often recited this nursery rhyme:

> *I have two little hands so soft and white*
> *This is the left and this is the right.*
> *Five little fingers standing on each*
> *So they can hold a plum or a peach.*
> *When I get as big as you*
> *Lots of things these little hands can do.*

"I've never been idle" were her words to me, and when she said them, I knew her current state brought her much sadness.

I can count the generations of my family in the Mormon Church back to the time of Joseph Smith and the origins of Mormonism, a continuous and connected whole. Then I count forward again until I get to me. This is where it stops. I've left the church and I've chosen not to have children—no legacy to pass on and no one to pass it on to. Although both of those decisions are right for me, I can't help feeling as if I've broken an essential connection. I never placed a grandchild into my mother's outstretched hands; we never stood apart, linked by the hands of a toddler between us. We never sat shoulder-to-shoulder in a church pew, hands entwined, mother and grandmother weeping proudly for the small child encircled by the men who would offer the gift of the Holy Ghost and a lifetime membership.

Over the years, I've searched for the peace and faith in the Mormon Church that the women before me carried with confidence. But I never found it. At age eight, two men lowered me into a warm pool of blue water to cleanse me of whatever sins my small soul might have accumulated thus far. The following day, four men rested their heavy hands on top of my small head to confirm my admission into the Church of Jesus Christ of Latter-day Saints. After that moment, I stuck close to the women in my family, seeking clarification and understanding of my position in this patriarchal society. But fifty years later, I could still feel the uncomfortable weight of those eight hands on my head. I left the church simply because the presence of men there was stronger than the presence of God.

As a child, I trailed my mother around the house, watching busy hands at eye level scribble out grocery lists, swipe dust off tabletops, and polish houseplant leaves. I was attached to her—often literally—clinging to a leg and reaching for those hands. I try now to visualize her young hands, but I cannot conjure up an image, only a sense of touch. I can feel the cool smoothness of my mother's fingers on the side of my face when she kissed me goodnight; I can feel the strength of my mother's hands in my hair as she twisted it into a ponytail; and I can feel the heat of her hands on my back when she pulled me toward her time after time to let me know that my father's wrath could not penetrate that hold. But when I try to *see* her hands, I can see only my own.

In first grade, I loved finger painting; I loved the visual and tactile sensuality of the paint. Maybe I knew then that I would outlive fluidly moving fingers, that the pleasure of touch would turn to pain. I feel as if I should have better prepared myself for this day, as if I should have braided my hair, opened all jars in the house, and photocopied a grocery list I could use in perpetuity so as not to force a pen into my aching hands.

But curling fingers never stopped the Hatch women from writing. They may have winced in pain as they scrawled words on paper, but I place my faith in the stacks of poetry, letters, stories, and genealogy occupying boxes in my basement, all written in the same scratched-out scribble of Ethel Gooch Hatch and her daughters.

I often riffle through the papers, feeling the weight of those stories in my hands. I make notes on a pad, not knowing where the notes will lead, but hoping they will lead to answers for which the questions have yet to form. I have been at this for years. The beginning notes are neat and legible, written in a sure hand. The notes written yesterday are less so, the lines crooked, the hand less confident.

Before my mother died, we dug through the boxes—then stored in her basement—together. During that time, we clung to each other as if we knew we were coming to the end of some-thing. With my decisions, I have ensured that what she and I shared—a connection that engulfs the love, strength, and sacrifice of six generations of Mormon women—will not be repeated. Lately, this does not sit well with me, but I'm not sure why. I am not longing for the child that never was, nor am I entertaining the idea of returning to the church. I have 32 first cousins with more than 240 offspring; there is little possibility that the Hatch/Gooch legacy will die out.

What I'm feeling is much closer to the bone. It resides within and between my mother and me. I am the beneficiary of the collective gifts—along with the limitations—of these women. Does that not carry with it some sort of obligation? To share, to pass along, to continue? Does it matter that I will cause a break in the chain?

As with my search for faith in the church, which I expected would present itself if given enough opportunity, so went my search for faith in motherhood. The two—motherhood and Mormonism—were inextricably linked in my mind. I had no model for one without the other. I don't know that I ever made a conscious decision not to have children. Instead, I waited patiently for the compelling reason to bring forth a child to clearly emerge from the amalgamation of fear, sadness, and anx-iety that occupied every small, empty space around me (this, also, an inheritance from the Hatch women). It never did. But now, since burying my mother, I am starkly aware that a piece of myself lies buried, a piece that can be accessed only through motherhood, a piece I will never know.

Yet, in many ways, it was this state of childlessness that gave room to the union between my mother and me. Had we turned our attention to a child in the middle stages of our relationship, would we have dug as deeply into each other? Would we have spent those many hours walking arm-in-arm through the gardens of the Mormon temple grounds, our heads tipped toward each other, our voices whispering those things we told no other person? Had I not left the church, had I not been searching for my reasons, would my mother and I have explored our shared history with such passion? Would I have learned that she, too, made unconscious choices from whence there was no return?

Ultimately, it was my mother's love and the cumulative fortitude of the women who came before me that gave me the courage to walk away from my historical legacy of Mormonism and motherhood. But there is sadness in this paradox; it tugs at me when I remember the feel of my mother's hand in mine.

In the rest home, when Grandmother could no longer lift her curled hand from the bed covers, she cried and pleaded with God to take her. One evening her children gathered. The four Hatch men linked their straight hands with the already curling hands of the four Hatch women and asked God to take their mother. They fasted and prayed until she died two days later.

When I first began to feel the pain in my thumbs and realized I would have the curled fingers of the Hatch women, I was horrified. But now, when I look at my crippled hands, I am reminded of the things the Hatch women have given me: compassion, perseverance, unyielding strength, a propensity to cry at every occasion, and a sense of humor to deal with my curling fingers.

My mother knew she would die before age eighty. Just a feeling, she said. She died seventy days before her eightieth birthday. As her organs began to shut down, I sat next to her bed and stroked her curled fingers with my own.

AFFORDABLE CARE

*We talk a great game of concern. We shout
at each other in high virtue, now more than ever
before, about the befoulment of our nest
and about whom to blame.*

—Lewis Thomas

About fifteen years ago, I experienced a yearlong period of loss—the end of a marriage, the loss of a home, separation from three dearly beloved cats that stayed with the home, the departure of three close friends, and a change of jobs. During that year I wallowed in fear and self-pity to the point of a minor—and clarifying—emotional collapse. Sitting in my Tucson apartment one day, staring out the window at the comings and goings of happy people in the small market on University Avenue, I experienced a palpable feeling of things being settled, for better or worse. I knew the period of loss had come to an end, but my life had relocated itself. The friendships would drift; the "I'm just a phone call away" promise of the ex-husband would not be acted upon. In that moment, I had a strong notion that I had to find my way to peace. I was nearing fifty and tired of my turbulent life, but having never before experienced peace, I had no idea what it might look like or how I might attain it.

I set upon building a life designed to restrict exposure to anything that would threaten my peace. I pulled my world in tightly, protectively. I moved to a small town, refused most social invitations—always emotionally fraught for me—and established myself as a not-to-be-bothered introvert. I did not get a cell phone; I did not tweet; I did not text. The world moved on without me. No one noticed—not even me—until, in another moment of clarity, I tried to unfurl myself and stretch my limbs, and butted up against the tiny structure of my phobic comfort.

I've learned in the years since that peace is not *attainable*. It's not something one acquires and has forevermore. It's a practice, much like yoga. Some days, a yoga practice flows smoothly, and one feels the bliss and fullness of the human body in movement. Other days, every posture is a battle of will between body and mind. Both practices—peace and yoga—require an act of letting go. Mistakenly, I presumed the longer I engaged in the practice of peace, the easier it would become, but that is not the case.

When I emerged from my cloister, I took a modern approach to reconnecting with the world: I joined Facebook. Yet, I don't feel at all connected. After twenty minutes on Facebook, I'm frazzled, the balance tipped, the peace obliterated. It's not the everyday banal posts that trouble me. There's something almost soothing about the photo of dressed-up deviled eggs with faces made of black olive and carrot bits posted by a "friend" I've never met. And the gorgeous goats, nothing makes me smile more. It means someone has found a way to care about this small source of delight in a world of beleaguering distress. What I'm having trouble *facing* in Facebook are the posts that shout: *Here's something you should care about, something you should be outraged by, something you should get involved in, something you should share*

*with others. Look! Care! Do something! At the very least, prove you
have a conscience by "liking" this post.*

Many posts are useful and informative, even laudable, which
is precisely the problem. I do care. But the moment I admit that,
I'm dumped back into the whirlpool and struggling with the
practice of peace amid the injustice, violence, and outrage that
circulates through an average day. Is it possible to live with both
peace and compassion? Is it possible to fill a life with joy and
beauty when daily notified of the destruction of beautiful places?
Can I continue to carry love inside me while being assaulted
with the death of it around me? In short, is my capacity for
caring vast enough to contain the magnitude of the demand?

In the last week, as in every week before it, a multitude of calls
for attention, money, and time crept into my life. They come
by e-mail, Facebook, phone, and a few in person. I counted
sixteen in one week not including those that I indirectly sum-
moned by reading the newspaper. One issue spawns another
issue. Environmentalism, poverty, racism, sexism, ageism, violence, healthcare, education, animal cruelty—every possible
topic brings with it a flood of legitimate concerns, a long list
of related injustices, and at least a dozen organizations trying
to stop the inequity and madness. If I respond to one organization, ten more contact me.

I'm overwhelmed by the competition for caring.

The problem is twofold. One, the opportunities for moral
outrage are plentiful, multifaceted, and urgent—many are
worthy of my energy. Two, I'm vulnerable to gravitational pulls
and prone to soaking up angst. If told that I am responsible
for this mess and guilty for that mess, I tend to believe it. And
every good organization for every issue, every advocate for every
worthy cause, plants a small reproach—maybe legitimately but

most certainly manipulatively—in the psyche of every person who turns away from the problem. How does anyone with a conscience navigate that minefield?

When a feral cat had a litter of kittens under my front porch, a friend told me that we are all morally responsible for the helpless critters that enter our lives. That's a lovely sentiment. But in my small town, where the feral cat population is higher than the human population and where dogs are regularly abandoned by people driving through a remote town that does not have even an old-fashioned animal shelter let alone a no-kill shelter and an army of animal advocates to offer assistance, it's also an extremely challenging and guilt-laden sentiment. But say one does decide to take on the full-time commitment of animal care in Escalante? What then happens when the next moral obligation—one of a few hundred possibilities—shows up?

Part of my care fatigue comes from sheer volume, but another part comes from our discomfort with uncertainty, our reluctance to pause. We no longer sit with issues, ponder them, question them, discuss them. We have no tolerance for letting thoughts develop and evolve. We dare not admit ignorance on any given topic; we dare not take the time to seek knowledge. When asked to take a position—no matter our level of understanding on the issue—it seldom occurs to us that we have the option not to. We're quick to take a stand and quick to take offense.

This, too, I suppose, is a result of our changing forums—the nifty nature of hiding behind computer screens and summarizing our thoughts in 117 characters or less. We don't have discussions; we have standoffs. And we're prone to flinging simplistic ultimatums: *You're either with us or against us! If you're not part of the solution, you're part of the problem! If you can't propose a different solution, you have no right to argue against mine!*

If you use electricity/drive a car, you have no right to take a stand against fracking/coal mining! If you don't vote, you have no right to be appalled by the unethical actions of politicians!
   Let us stop. Just for a moment. Let us stop manipulating, stop blaming, stop accusing, stop overgeneralizing, stop lying, stop giving ultimatums, stop threatening, stop demanding, stop fearmongering. Stop yelling. Stop screaming. Stop stomping feet and pounding fists. Please let us stop. Pause for a moment. Listen. Breathe.

   I was recently asked to contribute an essay to an anthology about water issues in the West, without a doubt, one of our most urgent issues. I like the idea of the book because it feels like an opportunity if not for discourse, at least for exploration, a sharing of thoughts and ideas. But the collection, the editor told me, would not have a "doomsday" tone. My contribution should be "positive" and should "propose solutions." That stumped me. I have no fix to offer, no cheerful notes to end on. Deep in my heart, on this and many other issues, I have a niggling feeling that we have arrived at a place without answers. But I could be dead wrong and would appreciate being proven so. And for that reason, I believe that rummaging through issues is worthwhile with or without a soothing solution.
   I suspect this inkling—that we may be out of answers— resides at an unconscious level in many of us, the fear of which adds to the vitriol of what can no longer be described as discourse. We're operating in crisis mode and the stakes are high. Life and death. If we run out of drinkable water, we die. If we don't have breathable air, we die. If we are unable to feed the mass of humanity we've created, we die. If we change our climate

to one that cannot sustain animal life, we die. And almost every issue—violence, poverty, racism, sexism—is interconnected to the competition, the pecking order for life-dependent resources. It's a volatile atmosphere of individuals, some filled with full-fledged panic and others with extreme denial. The deniers are angry with those who would disturb their delusions, and the panic-stricken are angry with those who won't join their calls of distress. I don't know if we are a good and cooperative species or if we are a ruthless and competitive species. I've seen examples of both, but the latter seems to be gaining an edge. And that, in my mind, makes the practice of peace vital.

If I want to spend fewer hours of my life being morally outraged, I must let go of more than I grab on to. Despite the great and worthy demands for my attention, I must be narrowly selective. I'm opting to take hold of what is near and dear—my community and the desert that surrounds it—because caring in a small, nontechnological way makes sense to me. It feels manageable. And it can be balanced with a practice of peace.

Some have called my decision a head-in-the-sand approach. I disagree. For one thing, I believe in peace. I believe it can spread from one person to another. I believe that more people committed to the individual practice of peace might result in more creative answers. At the very least it would cut down on the fury and noise.

The act of caring in a small local way feels embryonic, a single cell that has the capacity to divide and create more cells with specialized functions. Maybe those small cells of caring dotted across the earth can't help but bind into connective tissue, supporting the growth of healthy organs.

PROTECTED SPACE

*A well-managed solitary life, whether surrounded by
people or protected from people, is a very delicate and
a very difficult work of art.*

—John Cowper Powys

For some time now, I have been trying to understand my desire
for extended periods of solitude and my simultaneous thwarting
of it. I've been telling myself that my love of solitude comes
from an enlightened place, a contemplative place, maybe even
a superior place, which gives me the right to demand it. But
the longer I sit in solitude, the more conspicuous becomes the
spurious nature of my motives.

My solitude is not driven by virtue but by dread and disgrace. It comes from a patriarchal lesson repeatedly taught me:
any social situation—"social" defined as being in the company
of one or more human beings—is an opportunity for humiliation. I have closed myself around that message. When I walk
into a room with others present—whether one or one hundred—I feel my body, my heart, and my soul constricting. It's
a deep and palpable instinct, and going against instinct takes a
great act of will. I seldom succeed.

I am free when I am alone; I am fearless when I am alone.

*

One day, many decades removed from my father's emotional reach, I watched him direct his favored child-rearing technique toward my brother's youngest daughter. She had shamed him by being the oldest child—at about five—in a motel swimming pool using floatation aids.

"Get your water wings, little baby!" he called to her while striding the wet edges of the crowded swimming pool in cowboy boots and wrangler jeans. His belt buckle caught the sun at each turn. "Just like the two-year-olds. Maybe you need a diaper, too, little baby! Get your water wings!"

People looked up from their picnic lunches and romance novels to determine the cause of the ruckus. My mother and I were lounging on chairs out of splash reach in a far corner of the chain-linked rectangle. I put my book down and looked at her.

"Oh, I wish he wouldn't do that," she said. "It just breaks my heart."

I was wishing the same, but neither of us moved to stop him.

When I was the age of my niece, my father called me into the kitchen where he and my mother were entertaining friends. Fully aware of my fate, I sat on the stool beneath the yellow wall phone and fiddled with the cord.

"Say 'canyon,'" my father instructed. His eyes glistened, as if he were a proud parent asking a child to recite a poem or sing a song.

"Oh, Reese, for heaven's sake, leave her alone," one of the women—not my mother—said.

"Say 'canyon,'" he demanded.

"Cang-yun," I said.

He tipped his head back and cackled, then looked around the room ready to have his incredulity confirmed. My mother stared into the relish tray. The same woman who had spoken waved her hand and shook her head. I ran from the room.

Thirty years later, my mother and I both yielded to my father's talent and tenacity for public humiliation. We knew it would crumble us long before we rescued the child. My niece knew it too. She paddled to the middle of the pool and did an admirable job of ignoring him. When he realized she intended to stay there—and could because she was wearing water wings— he turned to a nearby stranger to explain that the child had had swimming lessons.

"For hell sakes, I don't think she'll ever take off those goddamn water wings!" he said with a hiccuppy sort of exaggerated chortle and a glance around the pool for support. When he found no takers, he stomped toward us. My mother and I buried our flushed faces in our books, but that didn't end his tirade on the embarrassing cowardliness of five-year-olds.

My father found this method of lesson delivery both effective and efficient. In addition to proper pronunciation, I learned most things—how to ride a bike and later a horse—with my father nearby, forced by his daughter's ineptitude to prostrate himself in public. It did, indeed, create a desire to learn quickly and cured me of any notion that I might want to play a team sport.

My father died eight years ago at the age of eighty-two. He was a miserable and pathetic man, but in some ways a very powerful man. I am still discovering the span of his reach.

Thwarting solitude is also something I learned from my father. He had a great fear of being alone for even an hour. Without continued substantiation from others he might walk into my mother's pink-tiled bathroom, look in the mirror, and see nothing at all. During the last sixteen months of his life— his lifespan beyond my mother's—he spent upwards of twelve hours a day sitting at the end of a broken-down loveseat next to a telephone and a Rolodex. The bishop of my father's Mormon ward told me that my father had called him four times on the day he died, and they talked for an hour each time. He had called me three times the same day. When the phone rang the fourth time I didn't pick it up or even look at the caller ID. When I checked the phone message many hours later, I learned that my father had been killed driving to the new Home Depot on the north end of his small town.

My mother liked to visit me during the many years I lived in Tucson. My father did not visit because I had cats. He accused me of having cats for the sole purpose of keeping him away, but that was not the only reason I kept cats. I like cats. Shortly after my mother would arrive, she would get a phone call from my father. He would say, "Apparently you don't love me anymore, apparently you love your daughter more than you love your husband, apparently I'm not good enough for you anymore, you have to go running off to Tucson. What am I supposed to do? Live on toast?" She would spend upwards of an hour reassuring him. This happened every day during her visit, often two or three times each day. When she hung up the phone, she would cry.

My mother craved solitude. On the rare occasions that my father left for a day or two to attend a cattle sale in a nearby state and my mother found a convincing reason to stay home—maybe a long-standing doctor's appointment—one of her children or grandchildren would stop by to check on her, to make sure she was okay. She hated that, but she didn't know she had a right to send them away. All the later years of her life, she waited patiently for my father to die, thinking she might live a few solitary years in peace. His father and a younger brother had died young of heart attacks, and my father was wound tightly. She had reason to be hopeful. Near age eighty, though, she gave up and died. Rest in peace, Mother.

I prefer to believe that I am more like my mother than my father, but that belief was easier to maintain when I was thirty than it is now. As I age, things work their way up to the surface like bones in the sand. My father's fear of solitude is in me, and as much as I carry my mother's craving for it, the fear often subverts it. Having been severely warned that to be old and alone is a horrible and inevitable fate, I have spent the last forty or so years warding off that cruel destiny. I don't particularly want a lot of friends at this point in my life, but I am fervently cultivating them nonetheless.

In his 1933 book *A Philosophy of Solitude,* John Cowper Powys argues that only those who have nurtured a strong solitary interior can endure society. "We have reached a point," writes Powys, "where the fallacy has been exposed that the increase of social intercourse and the apparatus of social pleasure does anything but murder real happiness."

I wonder if Powys had a father like mine.

Like Powys, I cannot conceive of *happy social beings*—those people who hang out in groups, who have upward of a thousand Facebook friends and dozens of walking, breathing friends; those people who chat on telephones to the tune of fifteen thousand minutes annually and send an astonishing twelve hundred texts a month; those people who stay *connected* to friends and family through every day and often every hour; those people who never have a thought that goes unexpressed or a moment that goes unshared. I cannot will myself to believe they are happy. I think they are faking it with every exclamation mark they type. I think they are skimming the surface of life, held afloat by a handheld device, never to breach the dark depths of their own souls.

Maybe I'm wrong.

Maybe exploring the depths of one's soul—something I've always placed a premium on because it must be done alone—is overrated. According to everything I read, see, and hear, there are not many people in the world (or at least in the English-speaking world) choosing solitude over company. *We're social beings!* shout the experts. *People with lots of friends and busy social calendars live longer, happier lives!* Maybe it's time for me to admit that there's joy to be found in the company of others.

But maybe not.

This year, I made a New Year's resolution to shut up. I want to be a quieter person. Two different friends (I have a few) when I shared this resolution asked, "Do you really think that's a good idea? To shut up?" Their questions made me wish I hadn't shared my thoughts, thereby providing empirical evidence in support of the resolution.

So much of what I say to others I wish I hadn't. I feel as if I've given a piece of myself away cheaply. When I am with another person, I often speak from a sense of civility, as if silence would prove me discourteous. But I like silence; I don't want to fill it gratuitously. In fact, I want everyone to adopt my New Year's resolution. I want most of the world to shut up. Imagine big public spaces filled with quiet people.

I realize that people can enjoy both company and solitude—but not in equal measure. We tend to favor one over the other. There is a part of me that does enjoy human company—albeit usually only one or two beings at a time—but it is a deeply protected part. It expects the worst from others and, therefore, often drives to that destination. I am bewildered but never surprised when friendships end. And maybe I'm not all that bewildered either. Just sad.

This part of me that wants the company of others is easily surprised by warmth and kindness and often does not know how to respond. By the time I figure it out, by the time I have cast about for the joke on me before concluding the gesture sincere, the warm, kind person is often gone, having sought but not having found an aperture in me.

In her slim book *Fifty Days of Solitude*, Doris Grumbach writes of her motives for insisting on time alone:

> My intention was to discover what was in there, no matter how deeply hidden.... If I dug into the pile of protective rock and mortar I had erected around me in seventy-five years, perhaps I would be able to see if something was still living in there. Was I all *outside*? Was there enough inside that was vital, that would sustain and interest me in my self-enforced solitude?

For years I aligned my solitary motives with Grumbach's. How honorable the journey of self-discovery, the search for the inner core of being. How worthy the act of pushing against the self created from the outside in.

The recent discovery that my solitary ways were created through degradation has jostled me. It has taken the righteousness out of my solitude and forced me to rethink my claim on it. Solitude without explanation or justification is a seditious demand in our society, especially for women. If a woman wants solitude in our hyperconnected culture, she must assert it with confidence and be certain in her motives. My motives have been exposed and called into question.

I've been asking myself if solitude is a form of hiding for me, a circumvention of a phantom threat, an avoidance of measuring myself against the well-performing crowd. The answer is yes, but I no longer care. Notwithstanding my nefarious path to solitude, I'm happy here. And I still believe in the virtues of solitude with or without virtuous motives.

I am not strong enough to hold on to myself for extended periods of time around other humans. Without solitude, I would suffer an absolute loss of self. If I don't have time free of the ideas of others, I do nothing more than absorb, react, and echo in whatever way I deem necessary for survival with minimal discomfiture. Solitude allows me to be a better partner to my husband and a better friend to my few close friends. Without solitude, I have nothing to give to a relationship.

I am no longer worried about loneliness in my old age. While I was sitting in solitude, it occurred to me that old age and loneliness, despite common wisdom, might not always arrive together. I might enjoy solitude at age eighty-five as much as I do now.

The reward of solitude is solitude.

CATCHING UP
ON MY READING

The only real influence I've ever had was myself.

—Edward Hopper

In my childhood home, reading was considered an act of indolence. Even now—years after burying my perpetually angry father and being closer to grave than cradle myself—reading a book feels dangerously insubordinate. Footsteps on the porch induce a moment of panic that has me stashing books between couch cushions and busying myself with a dust rag. When my husband enters the room and, by way of greeting, says, "Reading, huh?" I feel condemned. If I were Catholic, I would finger my rosary beads and hail Mary.

My childhood home contained one three-shelf bookcase built solely for separating front door entrance from living room. Tucked into its shelves were my father's high-school yearbooks, a few old economics textbooks, a history book about the Donner Party, the Bible, a hymnbook, and the Mormon triple combo: Book of Mormon, Pearl of Great Price, and Doctrine and Covenants. Stuck among those books were three novels: a tattered paperback copy of *All Quiet on the Western Front,* a first edition of *A Farewell to Arms,* which my mother later loaned to someone who never returned it, and a jacketless first edition of *A Tree Grows in Brooklyn.*

I remember the order of those books on the shelf because I was inexplicably drawn to them. I remember the padded and embossed covers of the yearbooks, the onionskin-thin pages of the religious books, and the yellowing pages of the novels. My mother never spoke of the books beyond once wondering aloud who neglected to return the Hemingway, nor did she encourage me to read them. The latter was, no doubt, for my own protection; she was the persistent, though ineffective, peacekeeper in our family.

I was once asked at a reading how I became a writer. My moment of confusion prompted the speaker to elaborate. "My daughter," she explained, "would like to be a writer, and I wonder if you might tell us the kinds of things you read from an early age, what helped form the writer, and what you might recommend to a young girl who wants to do what you do?"

First, I recommend that she not have a father like mine. Second, I recommend that if she does, she learns to lie well when asked the inevitable, uninspired writer questions: "Who were your early influences? Who are your favorite writers?" If she can lie her way out of that, she can write fiction.

I've been asked those questions at least a dozen times, and I've given a dozen different answers. Usually I name the author of whatever book I'm currently reading unless I'm reading trash, in which case I say Virginia Woolf. Woolf has not influenced nor inspired me so much as intimidated me, but all those words start with "in." Close enough.

I clearly recall only two books from childhood: *Where the Red Fern Grows* and *Charlotte's Web*. At some point in my grammar-school days they were assigned reading, which gave me carte blanche to sprawl in a chair in broad daylight with a book in my hands. I read both books many times, milking the assignment for as long as I could get away with it. Still, when my father found me sobbing over the death of Old Dan and Little Ann, he responded with: "For Christ's sake, put some boots on; I need help with chores."

Certainly those were not the only books I was assigned to read (although my school district was not known for producing literary scholars), but no one placed Lewis Carroll or Beatrix Potter into my young lap, no one curled up with me for bed-time stories, and no one placed me in a corner with a book as entertainment. Of that I'm sure. The woman's question was a good one: How did I become a writer?

My early, and maybe only, external influence was my father, which is why I became an accountant before I became a writer. Accounting was work that showed well—degrees, certificates, paychecks, and business suits—but it was not work that set-tled well. I went about it in a passionless way, never believing it could center a life.

The saving grace in this writer's past was not a collection of great books, good teachers, attentive parents, and literary dinner conversations. It was circumstance and parental neglect. My father intended to raise young ranch hands. But when I was six years old, a horse ran away with me on its back, and I devel-oped not exactly a fear of horses, but rather a fear of horses in the vicinity of my father. I had a similar experience with cows. A few years after the horse incident, a 4-H project steer dragged me across the pasture by a lead rope triple-wrapped around my hand and wrist before slamming me belly first into an irrigation Rain Bird sticking twelve inches above the ground, at which point my hand popped loose.

W. H. Auden once said that "the so-called traumatic expe-rience is not an accident, but the opportunity for which the child has been patiently waiting…in order to find a necessity or direction for its existence." My opportunity had arrived. My father never gave up on his intentions, but, after those two incidents, he focused mostly on his only begotten son, allowing me to escape on foot or bicycle until half past dark without raising a note of concern.

Through the combined blessings of ranch-hand ineptitude and parental inattention, I found my way to the town library, a creaky-floored structure of the classic revival style built in 1911 with a $5,000 Carnegie grant. Like all buildings of its era, it was stifling hot in the summer and frigid cold in the winter, and like all libraries of its era, it smelled of rotting paper. My house smelled like cow manure. I took an immediate liking to the library.

Each time I visited, I checked out the maximum number of books allowed, enough to fill a wire basket attached to bicycle handlebars. I stuffed them under my bed and read them all but never with so much absorption that I couldn't lend a vigilant ear for my father's footfall. I didn't care what I was reading; it was like drinking beer behind the haystack—the thrill was in the act of defiance.

Is that why I became a writer? To defy my father? Possibly. Fear is my default position in life; defiance is my willful response. I left Utah for New York City in the early '80s in defiance of the minimal expectations set up for me; I left Wall Street in the late '80s in defiance of the person I was becoming there. When I arrived in Tucson in 1988, I tried to register for a creative writing class at the University of Arizona because I wanted to write and was naive enough to believe I could. Before agreeing to let me in the class, the professor asked me for a writing sample. Upon reading what I gave him, he denied me entrance—for my own protection. I would be shamed and humiliated, he said, by my fellow classmates. To give me an inkling of what that might feel like, he explained in great detail—using many of my own words from the writing sample he held in his left hand while gesturing with his right—why I should walk away from his office and never again consider placing words on paper. He reminded me of my father.

When I returned two years later upon gaining acceptance to the MFA creative writing program, I found out that professor (who no longer remembered me or our impromptu workshop) was not entirely wrong. The other students—many of them male and twenty years my junior—quickly edified me on the paucity of my literary education, and they seemed to find joy in doing so. Although I had been reading gluttonously in the twenty-five years since leaving my father's home, I had also been reading aimlessly and ignorantly. In the MFA program, my reading deficiencies took on the sensation of a naked-in-public dream.

I have since forgiven those students because they were young and male and American (as was the professor minus the young part), so they could hardly be held responsible for their arrogance. And I have forgiven them because their petulance taught me something important: I have a right to write.

It is hard for me to trace my steps to becoming a writer, impossible for me to understand my insistence upon a writer's life while being shunted from it, or, even now, to proclaim with any sense of certainty *why* I write. In his book *The Soul's Code,* James Hillman argues that our bifurcated view of genetics and environment neglects "the particularity" of a person. In other words, according to Hillman, my desire to loiter by the ill-stocked living room bookshelf and in the stuffy town library might not have been driven solely by my cowgirl clumsiness;

it may be that I was born with the character of a writer. I like both the simplicity and the grandiosity of that idea.

Writing remains, for me, an act of defiance, a deep and necessary part of this writer's soul, and yes, probably an inherent characteristic of the particularity of me. I cannot say what books influenced me; I cannot speak with any authority whatsoever on the works of any great writer; I cannot hold my own among literary scholars.

My small writing shed, built in the far southeast corner of my property eighty-nine steps from my house, has room for only one bookshelf, which holds about three dozen books, the titles of which change according to my mood. Upon entry, my eyes naturally wander over the book spines. Most of them are not to be found in Harold Bloom's Western canon. Many of them are children's books; I don't attempt to analyze the whys of that too closely. *Charlotte's Web*, *Where the Red Fern Grows*, and my mother's copy of *A Tree Grows in Brooklyn* enjoy permanent occupancy.

My father, my well-read fellow MFA students, and the professor who tried to shield me from the disgrace of my own words stand on the small covered porch of my writing shed, hands in pockets, peering in through the screen door. Inevitably, one clears his throat in a scoffing sort of way, which starts a small mutiny in my soul. Then I sit down and begin to write.

WILD THOUGHTS

The most alive is the wildest. Not yet subdued to man, its presence refreshes him.

—Henry David Thoreau

One of the last conversations I had with my father took place about four years before he died and two years before he stopped speaking to me. During a visit to Tooele to see my mother, I had walked out to the corrals and was leaning against a pole fence watching a 2,300-pound black Simmental bull. The bull threw his enormous head and snorted as he lumbered toward me to reach the trough at my knees where my father had thrown fresh hay.

"He's been a damn good bull," my father said as he folded his arms over the top pole and placed a boot on the lowest. We were all a little wary of one another—the bull of us, us of him, and my father and I of each other. In one smooth, familiar movement my father lifted his sweat-stained American Simmental Association ball cap, ran a chapped, arthritic hand over his bald head, and replaced the cap. He then pulled a piece of alfalfa out of the manger and chewed on one end. I did the same.

"He looks like a good one," I said to my father. I found myself annoyed by his easy manner, his presumption that all was well between us. Our uneasiness with each other could be pushed aside for moments at a time but never really expunged. One of us would eventually take a jab at the other. This time it was me.

"What do you think about the reintroduction of wolves into the Rocky Mountains?" I asked ready for his answer, prepared for a rant about calves being killed, ranchers' livelihoods being threatened. The bull blew snot in our direction and spewed hay leaves into the wind as if to encourage us to end this conversation and move on.

"Oh, I don't know," my father said slowly. "I guess it always depends on whose ox is being gored, doesn't it?"

I chewed harder on my piece of hay, trying to regroup after this surprising show of ambivalence from a man who bristled at the mention of any word that could be even remotely linked to an environmental movement. Discussions of "wilderness" and "open space" sent his already high blood pressure soaring. The mention of reintroducing a known predator of cattle should have had him snorting like the bull.

"If you had asked me that question ten years ago when I was still running cattle up on the Manti-La Sal, I'd probably be more radically opposed to the idea. But I sort of feel like they belong out there. I guess that's not much of an answer to your question, but I just don't know."

I raised my eyes from the cracked leather of my father's cowboy boot propped next to my frayed sandal, and in my peripheral vision I saw the profile of his weathered, age-spotted face. Over the last decade—starting about the time he turned seventy—he had sold off about two-thirds of his land and cattle. He never had a large operation to begin with and kept only enough to make sure he could still call himself a rancher. About forty head still wearing his Rafter R brand grazed on about two hundred acres of mostly juniper and rabbitbrush in Rush Valley,

Utah, a few miles south of where we stood at the corrals behind my childhood home.

My father and I watched the bull silently—his large jaw worked steadily and his broad back flinched routinely to clear flies. We were great arguers, my father and I, of the decades-old ranching-on-public-lands-versus-environmental-issues debate. When President Clinton designated the Grand Staircase-Escalante National Monument we could barely be in the same room with each other. But every so often we would reach an impasse, such as this one regarding wolves, brought about by finding ourselves too close on an issue.

My father broke the silence. "The problem is that there are just too damn many people, and humans tend to think they can manage everything and they really don't manage things very well."

On those points my father and I were in absolute agreement. And that is where I got stuck on the wolf reintroduction issue: wolf management plans. The management plans speak of wolves in terms of tourist dollars they might generate weighed against the economic losses they might create through natural predation. The management plans anticipate the numbers of deer and elk that might be hunted and killed by wolves, thereby usurping the rights of humans to hunt and kill the same, pondering whether human hunters must somehow be compensated for their losses. The management plans equip wolves with a transmitter to track their movements. I understand the necessity of wolf management plans if the wolf is to have any chance of survival at all in the Rocky Mountains, but the idea that humans can or even should attempt to manage an animal as beautifully wild as the wolf, as if nature were just another theme park to be carefully controlled for our amusement, rankles me.

Meanwhile, the one thing we refuse to manage is ourselves. The fact that the human species is reproducing exponentially while living in a habitat with finite resources has barely taken hold in our minds. Some scientists estimate that in the wake of this march of humanity we are now experiencing extinction of species at a rate from one hundred to one thousand times higher than in prehuman times.

The wolf provides us a perfect example of how each species we remove reverberates through the ecosystem in ways that we cannot possibly predict or correct. Research shows that wolf reintroduction in Yellowstone National Park has led to the stabilization of elk herds and an increase in grizzly bears, foxes, ravens, magpies, bald eagles, and golden eagles. And because of changed elk grazing patterns when wolves were reintroduced, it has also led to an increase in riparian willow areas and restoration of aspen groves, which have not regenerated themselves since the 1920s, about the same time the wolves disappeared.

In our pursuit of happiness and the American dream—something I have pursued as enthusiastically as the next person—our unchecked and unconscious extermination of other species has degraded and destabilized a complex support system that cannot be tilled and replanted like our backyard gardens. As far as I can see, this puts us dead-on a path of self-destruction, and until we experience a shift of collective consciousness that allows us to find our place in the cycle of nature instead of perceiving ourselves as nature's manager, I worry we will stay on that path.

A few months ago, a generous run of clean, red sand through slickrock seduced me to pull off hiking boots and thick wool socks. I stepped tenuously at first, then sank my left foot up to the ankle into cold sand while my right foot found the smooth stone. I was barely aware of the articles of clothing that followed the boots and socks because that's what nature does—calls forth our own human nature in its purest form. To the best of my knowledge, that sort of fusion with the natural world might be the only way to get to the core of ourselves. And I'm afraid that's what we risk losing—that essential capacity to tap into our own animal nature—if we cannot find a way to let the wild run wild.

Until then, however, we are left with wolf management plans and other small steps of redress. For the unfortunate truth is, the wolf must play by our rules. Wolves will be allowed to survive as long as they do not encroach upon the ever-expanding territory of humans the way we have shamelessly encroached upon theirs.

Less apparent, and possibly more urgent, than the reverberations through the ecosystem are the reverberations with each loss through the collective spirit and character of humanity. And it is that—that indefinable twinge in the gut, that longing you cannot verbalize, that hardwired human connection to what remains wild on this earth—that made my father drop his head a little closer to the fence post and speak softly about wolves.

THE HUMAN INTRUSION

The defense of living Nature is a universal value. It doesn't rise from, nor does it promote, any religious or ideological dogma. Rather, it serves without discrimination the interests of all humanity.

—E. O. Wilson

One recent summer, I left my desert home because an old friend invited me to her home in the Catskills. I hadn't seen her in twelve years, reason enough to vacate my dry and thirsty plot of land and suffer the repugnance of air travel. I had missed her easy laugh, her love and knowledge of books, and our shared neuroses. And, she dangled the promise of greenery, always a respite for a desert dweller.

The view from the farmhouse upstairs bedroom to which I was assigned proved well worth risking the lives of my water-dependent herbs and tomato plants in Escalante. It was, simply stated, green. Green upon green. Green behind green. Green in such magnitude a desert dweller might find it monotonous, almost crushing in its closeness.

I have never lived in such a place. I've been a desert dweller for all but three misguided years of my life so I was unable to explain the nostalgia that flushed through me upon arrival. But as synchronicity would have it, I found my answer within the pages of the only book I carried on that trip: E. O. Wilson's *The*

Creation: An Appeal to Save Life on Earth. In it Wilson writes about biophilia, the savanna hypothesis, and the evolutionary principle of preferred habitat developed by George H. Orians and Judith H. Heerwagen. When given a choice, says Wilson, people of different cultures, countries, and backgrounds overwhelmingly look for three characteristics when choosing a place to live: a *height* from which they can look out over a *parkland* with scattered trees near *water.* In other words, says Wilson, "habitats resembling those in which our species evolved in Africa during millions of years of prehistory."

I've always been a desert rat—the desert crawls through me and I crawl through it—so my first instinct is to argue with Wilson. But in that moment I could not deny the deep emotional tug I felt standing at the window looking out over the grasses, the woods, the creek. I felt the wistfulness of home in a place I'd never been before.

The principle of preferred habitat might explain why we westerners, even after living here through seven or eight generations, continue to strip the land around our homes of native cactus, sagebrush, and juniper and supplant them with lawns and trickling water features, both of which are nonsensical in the arid West.

The view from the farmhouse window: A tamarack tree gently spreads itself upward and outward at least fifty feet tall and twenty feet wide from its trunk in every direction. Fifteen feet up, the slender trunk splits, and two trunks grow side-by-side, equal in proportion, equal in production, a perfect partnership. I don't know if trees have identifiable genders, and I don't care to look it up, preferring to immerse myself in the essence of the thing. This tree is female. Not a hard, athletic female, but a soft, lithesome female. A rare female without insecurity or conceit.

I don't know much about trees. I spend a good amount of time outside, but my ignorance about the nature of things is generally widespread. Information seeps in and leaks out in equal parts, and I don't care. I just want to *be* in a place. I'm afraid I would be a disappointment to Wilson, who believes that if we were all better educated about the workings of the natural world, we wouldn't find ourselves in the mess we're currently in. I'm sure he's right.

Beyond the tamarack's wispy tendrils and tiny cone baubles, the thick lawn runs out to meet a tall-grass meadow and trees, mostly hemlock and syrup-bestowing maple. Gardens sprout pink and white peonies, purple lupine and iris, lavender fox-glove, orange and pink poppies, yellow sundrops, and white wood anemone. Near the vegetable garden, a stinky, as-of-yet unidentified bush sporting creamy, swaying feathers turns away plant-seeking deer. A slow, dark creek snakes through the yard and into the woods. The nostalgia of prehistoric recognition makes me want to lie in the meadow and weep.

Birds come and go from the tamarack paying me no mind. They don't admire us the way we admire them. They don't keep a people journal to jot down where and when they spotted a particular type of person sporting certain colors and singing a recognizable song. With few exceptions, says Wilson, almost everything in nature can survive without humans, the exception being three species of body and head lice. Humans, on the other hand, need almost every species on the earth for our survival— especially the insects—though we are loath to admit it. Wilson is too polite to say so, but when it comes to "living Nature," we are defiantly ignorant, and we protect our ignorance with gusto.

According to my two housemates, there are good birds and bad birds, desirable birds and undesirable birds, but I can't tell the difference. For the most part, all birds look pleasant to me, though one particularly large and confident blue jay throws its weight around at the bird feeder. I assume it belongs in the undesirable category, which I confirm at dinner. "Blue jays?" I ask. "They're assholes," is the response, a widely agreed-upon characterization that makes me giggle for its sheer humanness. But this bird sports a handsome crown and gorgeous deep blue, almost periwinkle wings and tail etched with gray and white design work. No wonder he's cocky. Yet he's common. The rarer the bird, the more desirable the bird, which explains why most humans are undesirable: We are not nearly rare enough.

The scent of the Catskills mountain air blowing gently through the lace curtains into the upstairs bedroom is unknown to me. The woods of the West never fail to catch my heart with their pine-infused, dry-rotting mustiness and dirt, and I could tell by watching my friend upon arrival that the woods of the East catch her heart in the same way. The smell here is more alive, coalesced and smoother, like a perfectly mixed cocktail with a little froth on top. The smell in the West is a shot of tequila followed by a shot of vodka followed by a shot of whiskey, strong and distinct. Maybe the difference can be attributed to the spacing of plants; I can't smell bare dirt here.

The sound in the Catskills is also unfamiliar. Birdsong rules the airwaves. Clear, vibrant, and contained as if the woods keep the sound near. In the open space of the West, the birdsong escapes, always in the background instead of the foreground. I'm most startled by the absence of a sound of summer that I have taken for granted my entire life: the *tish-tish-tish* of irrigation sprinklers. From the time I was born until I was in my late twenties, I fell asleep each summer to that sound. It soothed me. When I first moved to the city, I thought the urban noise was the cause of my insomnia, but it didn't take long to realize that I was missing my nighttime lullaby. The song returned when I moved to Escalante, and although I am now aware that it's a swan song rather than a lullaby, it still touches the dreaming child in me.

One evening I and my housemates sat on the porch of the art studio built in the woods next to the creek and caught glimpses of the setting sun through the trees, a somewhat frustrating experience for someone used to wide horizons. It felt like sitting in the back row at a music concert where the stage can be seen only occasionally between bobbing heads. But there's something comforting in the way that place repairs itself around the human intrusion with such abundance, such luxuriance. Makes a person feel welcome.

The arid West does not accommodate us so easily. It does not have the capacity to fill in around human intrusion in a few seasons or a few decades. The land around my Escalante home appears spectacularly tough—reddened and baked rocks, jagged, running cliffs, deep gulches exposing rocks more than 270 million years old, Entrada sandstone goblins and arches—the quintessential picture of the rugged West. But it is not tough. It is an extremely fragile ecosystem, and each day the degradation from human intrusion becomes more apparent. I feel lucky to live amid such beauty, but it can break your heart. We have damaged it beyond repair—there is no doubt about that—and we remain defiantly ignorant about the consequences.

Lately, there's been a discussion about coal extraction near my home and very near Bryce Canyon National Park. The proponents of tearing into two thousand acres of public land to extract coal have promised to "rehabilitate" the place at the end of thirty years of destruction. Such a promise is both laughable and sad. Cleaning up toxic air and water is the simple task. How does one put rocks back together after they are blasted apart? How does one replace animals (including humans) killed in the process? How does one rebalance the native insects?

The loss of insects would, of course, be laughed out of any discussion about the pros and cons of coal mining. We seldom hear environmentalists arguing on behalf of insects, yet close to 50 percent of all insects are endangered due to human intrusion. Once we lose insects, we lose flowering plants because we have no pollinators. We lose herbs and trees and shrubs, including fruit trees. We lose birds that prey upon foliage, fruits, and insects. We lose more insects that turn soil and ready it for planting. The natural ecological balance is not only a beautiful thing to the human, it is a necessary thing.

"We have only a poor grasp," says Wilson, "of the ecosystem services by which other organisms cleanse the water, turn soil into a fertile living cover, and manufacture the very air we breathe." In other words, every species we lose, even an ant, nudges us toward our own demise. Yet, we continue to toy with the delicate balance of nature like children playing with matches, like drunken teenagers playing Russian roulette. The boast of "rehabilitating" the land back to a pre-mining stage represents a perfect combination of hubris and gullibility. We believe it because we want to believe it. We want to believe we can have benefits with no costs. Defiant ignorance.

From the desk in the Catskills farmhouse bedroom, I hear the gurgle of the "tiny creek" that runs through the woods. That's the way the owner of the house described it: a tiny creek. The tiny creek runs deeper and faster than the Escalante River crossing I encounter on my daily walk around the circumference of my town. At the west end of Escalante, I trundle down the powdery banks of the river and cross without hesitation and without getting wet. The water level fluctuates but often comes no higher than the soles of my shoes.

Further downriver, the Escalante widens and deepens as it picks up the creeks of the Aquarius Plateau until it theoretically feeds into the Colorado River. However, it can no longer reach that great rushing river. Instead the Escalante runs into the unnaturally still waters of Lake Powell, the backed-up bathtub of the Colorado River.

Glen Canyon Dam, which created Lake Powell, offers another striking example of brazenness and credulity, trading short-term results for long-term destruction. The sacrifice of Glen Canyon was only the beginning. The dam fundamentally changed the Colorado River from a raging, brown, silt-filled river into a clear, serene river carrying less than 10 percent of its pre-dam sediment, permanently altering the formations of the Grand Canyon and killing off native fish. Most people don't care. We prefer slow-moving, clear water to a raging, muddy river anyway (evolutionary preferred habitat?), we have a hard time empathizing with the Humpback Chub, and we are notoriously inept at thinking beyond our own lifespan.

The day I returned to Utah from the Catskills, the Escalante River crossing on the west end of town was dusty bone-dry, and much of Utah was on fire. By the end of June, more than 175,000 acres had burned. The neighboring states—Arizona, Colorado, and others—were also burning. The fire closest to my house had burned 8,200 acres and was 10 percent contained.

The skies were filled with smoke. My house was not in danger, but my soul and my psyche were. The fire was started by a spark from an ATV. At the time of my return, 393 out of 438 Utah fires had been human caused. In other words, 90 percent of the fires were unnatural.

People who don't care about the Humpback Chub care about fires because they want to go camping and fishing. They want to roast hot dogs and marshmallows over a campfire on the Fourth of July. They want to light sparklers and firecrackers. They want to ride ATVs and shoot guns that create sparks. As Americans, it is their right to do so. The line connecting the disappearance of the Humpback Chub to the smoke burning our nostrils is too dotted to follow, and we have no interest in connecting the dots anyway. Defiant ignorance.

Some work to repair the damage we've done. They reintroduce species—frantically trying to reestablish nature's balance—and make pleas to the powerful with a few successes and many failures. In the mountains above my home, native beavers, having disappeared to trapping, were reintroduced. They happily splashed around North Creek Reservoir for a few weeks before someone trapped them, bashed their heads in, and threw the bodies back into the reservoir—a clear statement to those who would dare attempt such acts as balancing the natural order of things.

Some will rise above such horrific details and keep working despite the unconditional violence directed at them. I admire those people, but it feels a bit like trying to carry the Colorado River in one's cupped palms. Holistically speaking, I have little faith in the ability of humans to manage nature. Even the most laudable kind of "nature management" seems close to an absurd idea, an idea borne out of the egos, and possibly the desperation, of humans. Yet I still believe in individual acts of redress, individual attempts to save the living environment, which is nothing less than a very commendable attempt to save ourselves. Maybe those small balancing acts will make a difference. Maybe it is my own defiant ignorance—rather than the smell of burnt earth—that tests my faith.

THE MONSOONAL FLOW

OF KINDNESS

There is no need for complicated philosophy....
The philosophy is kindness.

—Tenzin Gyatso, the Dalai Lama

Monsoons have arrived in Escalante. Brash, vociferous storms carried into town on raucous winds and dumping fat, lavish globs of rain. As I write this, lightening flickers and thunder bellows. Clear water falls from the sky, one minute battering insistently, the next descending gently. Squishy mud forms around the porch of my writing shed as if it were the gift I've been waiting for. And it is.

We're in the third week of a good monsoon season. Those whose job it is to predict and report the weather call them *violent* storms. I call them kind, benevolent storms. My phone was deadened for a day and the water ran urine yellow from my kitchen faucet for a week. But I wouldn't call the loss of modern conveniences acts of violence.

Someone will surely point out that such storms *are* violent because they can be, and often are, deadly. In a nearby town, a young man was struck and killed by lightning during a recent storm, and hikers have been killed in flash floods, common in nearby canyons. But death itself does not denote violence.

Violence requires intent. And monsoons are just monsoons, there's no intent involved.

One could argue then, if monsoons cannot be violent nor can they be kind and benevolent. I suppose that is true. Monsoons are indifferent to humans, but I am not indifferent to monsoons. I choose to receive them as kind. After a summer start of scorched earth, smoke-filled air, empty lakes, disappearing rivers, and a dry, dusty yard—a stark preview, no doubt, of summers to come—I can't find anything but kindness and compassion in the storms. Others are free to receive them as they wish.

> *We have no room for suspicion when our hearts*
> *are filled with love.*

—Tenzin Gyatso, the Dalai Lama

Before the monsoons began, Steve and I attended a gathering in Boulder, Utah, of about fifty people interested in a new collective consciousness, a consciousness that would reconnect the human mind to the reality of the human habitat, a consciousness that would remind us that humans can live without fossil fuel, airplanes, and cars and have done so in the not-too-distant past. But humans cannot live—and never have lived—without clean air, pure water, and nontoxic food. Because a physiological adaptation to such a state is unlikely, most of us know—if we are conscious at all—that the choice among those things is quickly approaching.

As one might expect, based upon who has the most to lose in the game of chicken we're playing with the earth, the average age of those in attendance was approximately twenty to thirty years my junior. The crowd was hip, young, smart, and creative, and it showed in their manner of dress, in the expansiveness of their art, and in their relationships to one another. I felt the opposite of all those things: old, dowdy, out of place, and shunned. Steve—a redneck hippie intellectual who is comfortable in his own skin and, therefore, comfortable in any group—fit right in. For five days, we camped among the youth, sharing meals and conversation. It was not easy to keep my defenses up for a full week, but I managed.

On the final day the group came together to bid one another farewell with a few words from each of us. I had nothing to say, so while others spoke, I occupied myself with formulating something simple, something that wouldn't give me away as the only person who had not been transformed by the experience. But I kept getting distracted by the words of others, words that contained what seemed a genuine outpouring of love, not only for everyone in the room but for humanity and all life in general.

When it came my time to speak, I could not. While everyone patiently waited, I wept. A young man—a burner (a devotee of Burning Man) in his early twenties with wildly free, shoulder-length hair and face paint—sat next to me on the floor. As I attempted to speak through tears, he reached over, firmly wrapped his large hand around my forearm just above my wrist, and held on to me until I stopped crying long enough to mutter a few words. Afterward, as everyone stood to leave, I touched his arm and thanked him. He smiled big and engulfed me in a tight hug.

I don't know his name, I doubt I will ever see him again, and I don't know that I would recognize him if I did. But he taught me something about myself: I contain my own segregation. I

carried it into that gathering and at the moment of my vulnerability, the moment I let my guard down, he slipped in a
simple act of kindness.

*We have a need for others' kindness, which runs
like a thread throughout our whole life.*

—Tenzin Gyatso, the Dalai Lama

A while back, the *New York Times* published an essay of mine
in which I shared my lifelong struggle with fear. In the online
comments, some scoffed, some called me foolish, and some
argued that I have no right to fear. They pointed out that I live
in a beautiful place and that I have a tall husband and a cat,
thereby proclaiming me unworthy of fear. I agree. That's precisely what I tell my fear every morning: I am not deserving of
your presence.

Others urged me to hang on to my fear, even suggesting I
may not be fearful enough, especially when it comes to my physical surroundings. They conveyed the same message as does the
signpost that graces the trailhead near the Escalante River: You
Could Die Out Here! Precisely why wandering a vast, magnificent desert calms a person like me.

Many more readers—online and through e-mail—reacted
with the simple philosophy of kindness. I was stunned, perhaps
naively so, by the sheer number of such messages I received.
Some called me courageous for sharing my fear in a public way,
informing me that fear and shame often operate as a pair, and,
indeed, that was the message of the angry readers: *you should be
ashamed of your fear.* Some wrote to me of their own struggles

with paralyzing fear, irrational fear, fear that greets them every morning and haunts them throughout the day. Fear, it turns out, is democratic—it is not gender specific, it is not geographically specific. It does not care about skin color, sexual orientation, class, religion, profession, trade, talent, intellect, friends, family, love, or income level. No one is deserving of that kind of fear.

There will be obstacles on the way to developing
a genuinely warm heart.

—Tenzin Gyatso, the Dalai Lama

The other day, a friend of mine won an award for her recently published novel. I sat down to write her a note of congratulations, but it took me several days to work through my envy and irrational rivalry before I could put words down with sincerity.

My father, a miserly man, had a heart filled with grudge, leaving no room for generosity or humility. I am my father's daughter. I am the obstacle blocking my own path to a warm heart. Each day I set about remolding that weighty organ, knowing that the clay has dried and hardened, knowing that I'll have to take a chisel to it. As a child, I did not learn that joy can be shared, that there is plenty to go around. I did not learn that one person's good fortune does not supplant another's. I did not learn that opportunities for joy can be squandered. I am only just learning that if I don't carry kindness in my soul, I have no way to receive it from others.

Steve likes to run in the desert; I like to walk in the desert. Both of those things are made more pleasurable by the kindness of monsoons so we've been going out often, starting at different points and meeting in the middle. We typically go out after the monsoon has passed but the remnants linger: pools, quicksand, the scent of sage, and, if we're lucky, waterfalls over slickrock. Sometimes we're out when the monsoon arrives, so we tuck under an alcove to watch the storm through wide eyes and a panel of water or climb to the safety of high ground and squat under our rain slickers to watch the river rise, turn muddy, and gush below us.

Washed-smooth and moisture-packed sand is bliss to walk on—like walking on a sponge. It requires no trudging. As I walk, I can't stop myself from turning to look back at my footsteps, especially if I'm walking barefoot. I'm fascinated by the way they follow me, teasing and fun, a playful, existential game with a moral I've yet to figure out.

Once while walking together in post-monsoon sand, I noticed that I, in my slighter and smaller body, was leaving deeper prints than Steve. I attribute this to his lightness of spirit, his practice of casting off gratuitous millstones. I, on the other hand, encircle my neck with an albatross necklace, which I wear self-righteously to the point of cutting off my own breath. But as I age and carve away at my flinty self, I expect to one day turn and see only flush, pink sand behind me.

I watch Steve closely, trying to copy his technique. Some—those who don't know him well—might describe him as aloof, but he's deeply caring. So caring that he never tries to rescue me from myself, never tries to push me out of my own way. The depth of his kindness brings me to tears.

THE SHARP POINTS

There's no problem with being where you are
right now.

—Pema Chödrön

About six miles north of Escalante, just over the cattle guard on the road that goes to Posey Lake on the Aquarius Plateau, a trail on the right cuts across Pine Creek and winds a quarter-mile through sage and juniper before snaking directly up the mountainside. From the pullout, the high, steep ridge discloses no obvious route. Once it starts up the craggy, red- and white-faced rock dotted with vegetation, easy-to-miss rock cairns offer guidance in navigating turns and twists on a kaleidoscopic trail of red, orange, and purple splinters of shale—slippery when wet or dry. The trail climbs steadily for two miles before depositing a hard-breathing hiker on the top at a place called Antone Flat. From there, one can stroll through juniper and ponderosa to the edge of the world and peer into deep, endless canyons of slickrock.

Because it is short and close to town, I could hike it daily, and if I were of a Buddha nature, that would be the wise thing to do. Steep, slippery, and easy to lose, the trail requires strength, endurance, balance, and focus. Once you have all of those working, it sets up the perfect Buddhist paradox: at the same time it demands focus, it requires letting go, getting out of the mind, trusting the foot to find its place, trusting the animal instincts you were born with. It requires comfort with shifting ground and uncertainty. I believe the Roundy Trail to be a path of enlightenment.

The other day I decided to hike to Antone Flat when it seemed I had none of the requirements on hand. There are closer, easier trails when one is feeling like a semiattached piece of rusted sheet metal banging repeatedly against the shed in the wind. But that's where I found myself.

I tightened bootlaces, skirted along the barbwire fence down a washed-out gully, splashed through the creek, and stumbled across the desert floor through anthills larger than my kitchen table until a rock cairn alerted me to cut in and start the climb. As I settled into the ascent, I attempted to empty my mind. The contents do not go willingly. That's not to say that my mind is filled with important data. It's more like the kitchen garbage that is three days beyond when it should have gone out, filled with stinking waste and buzzing with fruit flies—full of lies I tell myself, imaginary conversations with real people, real conversations with imaginary people, useless *essential* information, fantasies, nightmares, scenarios worked out in all sorts of ways. Endless noise.

All of that is a good thing if the intent is to arrive at Antone Flat without being distracted by sweeping views of earth and sky, without noticing your pounding heart, without sensing cactus needle punctures and trickling blood. It's bewildering to walk through such habitat without experiencing it. Having reached the top in such a state, I sensed a missed opportunity.

The trip down, though, forced the issue. I started out clumsily, still engaged with the noise in my head until I tripped and skidded far enough down the trail to scare myself quiet.

Before the buzzing could start again, I dropped into a crouch-step, moving quickly, skating over floating pieces of shale. Instinctively, I regained balance after every slip. Impressed with myself, I maintained this zone for a good five minutes before being brought up short at a cliff edge, greeted by wispy strands of cirrus clouds at eye level. How long since I'd seen a rock cairn? I sat down, dangling my feet over the cliff edge to give it some thought.

If I choose to look closely at my motivations, which I don't often choose to do, I would guess that I found myself on that path on that particular day because it most closely resembled the day's happenings: the ground shifted under my feet, rock cairns disappeared, and danger lurked nearby.

Buddhist nun and author Pema Chödrön suggests that we cause our own suffering by relentlessly searching for solid ground that simply isn't there, by incessantly clinging to disappearing markers as the next storm rolls in. Of course, she's right. I've clung to one buoy after another looking for the final flotation device. Whether it be financial, emotional, or physical security, I want my lifetime warranty. Then I can stop holding my breath and go about life in a relaxed and cheerful sort of way.

We are a society of guarantees, promises, contracts, assurances, pacts, treaties, and pledges. Till death do we part. Never mind that the foolishness of this approach is flung back at us daily in the form of divorces, lawsuits, broken promises, bankruptcies, lapsed warranties, broken hearts, and suicides. Some of us would even like to be assured beyond death, so others have taken it upon themselves to offer such a thing. We shall not be dissuaded in our march toward *security*.

Chödrön proposes that we might instead want to cultivate a level of comfort with impermanence and uncertainty since that seems to be what life offers. "Lean into the sharp points" of life, she says. Instead of attempting to encase our hearts in something like a little pocket protector, we might do the opposite—unwrap our hearts, open them to pain and suffering, expose what she calls "the tender spot." From that piercing of the heart, she claims, comes compassion and light, a relaxation into today's reality instead of a grasping at tomorrow's illusion.

Radical. Logical. Difficult to implement.

But I'm trying it out. I've been meditating twenty minutes a day—not as easy as it looks—but I worry (a non-Buddhist thing to do) that amid all this loving-kindness I will become too appeasing, that my writing will lose its edge. One of the roles of an essayist is that of contrarian, and I love that role. It's the "opportunity to bristle" says essayist Phillip Lopate. When I voice my concerns to Steve, he assures me that I will never be conciliatory. I'm not sure whether that is a compliment or an insult, so I let it go without judgment (a Buddhist thing to do).

I wandered the hillside that day until I stumbled upon a rock cairn, then continued my slide down Roundy Trail, trusting the flow of groundlessness. As I did, I thought about letting go of my husband as security guard, as guarantor of my happiness, as permanent sentinel of my heart and well-being. Maybe we can show each other more love, more kindness, and more compassion if we let loose the security strapping. Maybe we can live more presently, allow for more spontaneity and playfulness, joy and passion, if we are not busy demanding promises of, and making promises to, one another.

This will take time and practice. Letting go of security—even if it's only an illusion—creates a feeling of, well, insecurity. But I've already let Steve go as far as the post office without first promising to love me forever. Tomorrow, we'll try the grocery store.

MOVING WATER

The places where water comes together
with other water. Those places stand out
in my mind like holy places.

—Raymond Carver

The summers of my single-digit youth were spent exploring—
in both directions and in glorious oblivion—the creek that ran
on the far side of my backyard's chain link perimeter in Tooele,
Utah. Beyond the creek, open wheat fields housed a large population of the horned lizard known to us as horny toads. The
front yard represented civilization: lawns, curb and gutter, side-
walks for chalk-drawn games, and paved roads for bicycling. I
had my pick of worlds—wild or tame—and I indulged in both.

The ditch, as we called it, was about four feet wide and maybe
a foot deep in most places. It had a good flow. Into the water,
my best friend and I dropped all things—plastic balls, sticks,
leaves, paper boats, stuffed animals, children's books, and dolls—
to check the item's floatability, the water itself holding more
wonder and entertainment value than the item we dropped.

Once we detected a good floater, we'd launch it, rush out front
to our waiting bikes, and race down the sidewalk several blocks
before thrashing through pussy willows at the place where we
hoped to intercept floating Barbie before she went under the
road and disappeared for good. My enthrallment with moving
water has never diminished, though my access to it has.

A few years ago, while doing research for a novel centered around Southern Nevada Water Authority's plan to build a three-hundred-mile pipeline to gather water from Nevada's and Utah's deserts and deliver it to Las Vegas, I became shamefully aware of my ignorance on the subject of water. It's not much comfort, indeed none, to know that I have a great deal of company. I joke about those who believe the kitchen faucet to be the source of their water, but the reality doesn't stray far from the gag, making it more tragic than funny.

I might be less sheepish had I grown up in the lushness of upstate New York, the swamps of Florida, or the damp forests of the Oregon Cascades, but I grew up in Utah's west desert, although during my youth I never heard it referred to as such. Maybe I slept through geography classes, maybe I was distracted by the closeness of the boy at the next desk, or maybe my senses were dulled by the soothing sound of unfettered water nearby, but I was far into adulthood before Wallace Stegner's slim book *The American West as Living Space* educated me about my desert home and what it means to be a desert dweller.

I don't know whether to fault myself or the education system for the lack of geographic knowledge that followed me through life. Probably both. In his introduction to *The Sound of Mountain Water*, first printed in 1985, Stegner writes, "In most parts of the West (Utah is one exception) a child is likely to learn little in school about the geography and history of the region that is shaping him. He gets them through the pores if he gets them at all." I take exception to Stegner's exception. I am living proof that Utah fit the educational mold of which he writes. What geographical knowledge I've acquired over the years has, indeed, come through the pores.

One hot summer day between second and third grade, my friend and I hatched a plan to follow our ditch upstream, an adventure of such great proportion, I felt like Nellie Bly. We had no destination in mind; I'm chagrined to admit we had no idea where the water would lead us. Unbeknown to us, we began a journey in search of the ditch headwaters.

I consider myself lucky to have grown up in an era of mothers who sent their young into the town wilds fully expecting they would reappear at sundown. I find good reason to wax nostalgically about those less fretful times. 'Twas sweet luxury to be beyond a parent's reach for the span of a summer day at the age of eight.

We traveled with domestication on our left and wilderness on our right, the creek providing a line of demarcation between the two—a scene my eight-year-old self took for granted, a static world where creeks and wheat fields don't disappear in two years' time. We hadn't gone more than a mile before stopping for lunch amid willows, having spent most of our energy in the plotting phase of our daring quest. Although the sun was high and hot when we pulled our feet from the creek and laced up our Keds, I suggested we turn back. *Better safe than sorry*—one of the worst slogans ever set in type—was my early philosophy of life. But my friend, the alpha female of our two-person team, wouldn't hear of it. We pressed on. I was considerably out of my comfort zone when we reached the cement plant on the south edge of town and near the point of panic upon reaching Highway 36 just beyond. We crossed the highway and paused at a wrought iron fence erected around a few pioneer graves, including several children, in the mouth of Settlement Canyon, an arrival so portentous in my mind I found myself near tears. Immune to my histrionics, she kept going, and I stumbled after her.

As we walked directly into the Oquirrh Mountains, a strange and lovely thing happened: the ditch, *my ditch*—the one that carried away toys and disappeared under paved roads and into concrete culverts—turned itself, as if by magic, into a mountain stream, a beautiful, gurgling flow that led us deeply into shadows of large cottonwoods, a cool darkness so enchanting it stripped me of breath and fears.

Less than a mile into the canyon, we stopped at a wide place in the creek, a canopy of branches and leaves above our heads, and a rough plank bridge across the water built seemingly just for us. We dangled our feet, waded and splashed, padded barefoot on the dusty banks, and laid on our bellies to slurp our fill of clear mountain water before starting home as the sun dropped.

It was my first serious romance with a natural place, a place that provoked yearning and dreaming, a place that churned the belly and dizzied the brain and unveiled a world of possibility. It was the first time I understood that open air, dirt, trees, and flowing water make up the natural habitat of humans.

We returned many days that summer and the summer to follow. We planned our lives, chose our husbands, named our children, and whispered our secrets as if the place itself would grant each fantasy and protect every confidence. We had slipped through a hidden chamber into our own enraptured forest.

Then it was gone. Bulldozed, stripped, destroyed, and flooded. In 1966, the year I turned ten, I witnessed my first western water project: an earthen dam constructed at the mouth of Settlement Canyon. I had heard my father—a man already in the plotting stages of buying a small ranch, a man who loved the sight of water spurting from metal pipes as much as I loved it cutting through the earth, a man who, in future summers, would give new meaning to the phrase "moving water," as in "we need to get that goddamned water moved"—talking excitedly about the dam. But never in my mind did I align the construction of the dam with the destruction of my place until it happened.

Certainly the flooding of the mouth of Settlement Canyon is a tiny blip of a thing compared to, say, the flooding of Glen Canyon, which happened around the same time. But my ten-year-old heart shared the depths of despair described by David Brower as he watched Glen Canyon fill with water in the years after the Glen Canyon Dam gates closed in 1963: wretched desolation for the loss; unfathomable disbelief that so many could accept it so easily.

As a sixth-generation Utah Mormon, I come from a long line of master irrigators, a great heritage of water movers. When Brigham Young said, as the myth continues, "This is the place," and shortly thereafter promised to "make the desert bloom like a rose," in true Mormon fashion, he girded his loins and went to work. Under his command, Mormons moved earth, built ditches and took water from mountains to valleys, insisting the desert produce crops it had never before considered. It would turn out to be one of the largest and most successful irrigation systems of its time and possibly the inspiration for many water projects that followed.

Every "water project," every large or small manipulation of water from its natural course, carries with it a loss. Whether it happens through damming and flooding, through pumping and draining, or through the urban development supported by such projects, a natural place is forever changed.

I knew nothing of the reasons behind the Settlement Canyon Dam at the time it was built. I only knew it had stolen *my place*, and to this day the tiny, still reservoir, accessed by a recently added tollbooth and gate, strikes me as one of the most repulsive places on earth, and it becomes more revolting and unsightly with each visit, as if the dam set into motion a decline from grass, trees, and water to concrete, beer cans, and used condoms. Promotional materials of the area publicize the reservoir's "unsurpassed beauty and recreational fishing opportunities," but beauty is a relative thing. One can see the beauty in a man-made body of water nestled into a valley only if one never felt the spirit of the place snuffed out by it. I suppose Lake Powell is beautiful to some who never saw what lies beneath. I am one of those who never visited Glen Canyon before the flood, but I've spent the last five years wandering the desert near Lake Powell, and my ten-year-old heart identifies the loss.

I've probably seen most every dam within a three-day driving distance of Tooele. My father, giddy with dams, often ordered us into the car to "go see the dam," whether that meant a short drive to check the water level in Settlement Canyon or an eighteen-hundred-mile drive to see Glen Canyon Dam, Hoover Dam, Davis Dam, and Parker Dam during one car trip. I don't know how common it was in the 1960s to create vacations around dams, but for us, Glen Canyon Dam was the destination, the Grand Canyon a side trip. I was duly impressed with the constructing prowess of my species.

The Settlement Canyon Reservoir, which collected and stored snowmelt and a spring-fed creek, not only took my sacred place but also ended my joyful play in open ditches, which soon thereafter disappeared followed shortly by open fields. Once we had a modern water system, we could "grow the town," build housing developments, and water lawns without restraint, and I've never met anyone else who felt that as a loss rather than something to celebrate. *Without restraint*, however, was a short-term dream now seeking new dreamers, a commonality among western water projects.

While researching the novel, I attempted to learn the intricacies of water, but my ignorance spreads like ditch water turned into a flat field. The issue of western water pulls in the complexities of nature, science, politics, law, history, economics, and psychology, and swirls them together in a deep bog. One soon becomes mired in the muck.

Environmentalists have their lawyers and lobbyists and scientists, cities and states and counties and water authorities have theirs, and agriculture and mining industries have theirs. Scientists' points of view often contradict one another, and others choose whatever piece of science fits their agenda, trusting that the convolutions of the issue will keep most interested parties confused and ignorant, a tactic that works quite well.

The history of water in the West is driven by economics and fraught with backdoor deals, greed, power struggles, and gargantuan foreseen and unforeseen—and mostly permanent—consequences. When it behooves us to trot out history we do so, which is what has given the agricultural industry a stronghold on western water for many years, and when it behooves us to ignore history—depleted aquifers, raised salinity content in freshwater rivers, disappearing native fish, invasive species, and the drying up of springs and native plants—we're quick to dismiss it.

History also drives psychology, as is the case in Escalante, where we run out of irrigation water every summer regardless of winter snowpack levels and despite the enormous cost of a newly constructed dam. Water users here operate under the *use it or lose it* policy. We water as if we are one of ten stepping up to a dinner table set for four. We get ourselves into a fighting stance and get as much as we can as fast as we can before it is gone, which, of course, guarantees that it will be soon gone, which in turn affirms the approach. Those who operate under this popular maxim think water conservation is a great idea— the more the neighbors conserve, the more I get.

Water causes a lot of snarling in the West, as will happen when animals compete for scarce, life-sustaining resources. After the Nevada pipeline plan was announced, one rancher from Callao, Utah, declared the pipeline a moral issue by proclaiming that the water shouldn't go to support Las Vegas lives of "glitter, gluttony, gambling, and girls," as contrasted with the apparently more deserving rural folks "personified by cattle, children, church, and country." Nevada's water czar growled back that the folks in Utah "can't even spell conservation." Both statements hold a sliver of truth deeply buried in a slice of sanctimony. In Utah we've internalized the directive to "make the desert bloom like a rose" as if it were God's eleventh commandment, shooting us up near the top of the list of per capita water consumers in the West.

I agree that construction of a three-hundred-mile pipeline to pump water from its natural course is, indeed, a moral issue, although not, as the Callao rancher would have it, one based on the goodness of rural residents. I don't believe a rancher living in Spring Valley necessarily holds the moral high ground over a card dealer living in Las Vegas. I assume the residents of Las Vegas are as devoted to their children, church, and country as are the residents of Callao. I see it as a moral issue based not on the character of rural versus urban residents so much as the character of the human species in general, a moral failing in refusing to acknowledge that we are not—and never will be— nature's controllers.

Water has its own nature. It cares not for the needs and whims of humans. It is not dependent upon us; we are dependent upon it—for our very lives. One might think that would make us humble in the face of nature and careful to maintain the balance that our lives depend upon. *How does man intervene?* the Nevada water czar asks and answers her own question this way: *The magic lies in managing that basin.*

We are a strange animal believing in our own cleverness in the face of evidence to the contrary. From the moment we began manipulating water in the name of civilization—yanking water from its natural course through pipelines, damming it, diverting it, wasting it, polluting it, and exhausting it before moving on to our next clever act—we have been rushing headlong toward the inevitable: a time and place where human cleverness runs out and nature pulls us up short. We have arrived.

Water projects have allowed western cities to grow beyond their natural capacities, and water projects have allowed agriculture to flourish in places agriculture should not exist or should exist only on a small scale. Las Vegas, Salt Lake City, Phoenix, Tucson, and many others have grown unrestrained in the middle of deserts that demand restraint. Now what? It is difficult to shrink a city whose economy is—as are all U.S. economies— based upon growth. It is difficult to close down a city and disperse its residents. It is difficult to prevent people from moving to the West, although the West cannot support more people. It is difficult to ask people to stop having children because we have no resources—especially water—for those children. It is difficult to demand that ranchers stop ranching, stop doing what they love, stop living the only way they know how to live, although it makes little sense to grow hay and graze cattle in the driest states in the nation.

Water projects allow us to live beyond our means, something red-blooded Americans see as a God-given right. *Live large!* say advertisers, lenders, corporations, universities, governments, parents, and churches. We take the idiom literally. The idea of living where we are, in the small space we occupy, is as foreign and horrifying to us as hauling a bucket of water from a creek for daily use.

When I talk to people involved in western water issues, I ask about population control. The question is invariably met with silence. It is the fat, lumbering elephant in the exceedingly narrow room, a political pariah, a conversation ender. Environmentalists won't discuss it because they will be marked as anti-family, anti-Christian extremists. Politicians won't bring it up for the same reason. Yet addressing, or at least discussing, the outbreak of humans and the ability of the earth to support the species is not only the obvious answer, but possibly the only answer. After scientists and politicians and lawyers are done processing and finessing the details, one simple truth remains: If we use water faster than it can be replenished, we die.

The earth has finite space and finite resources upon which life depends. The lack of our inability to hold that truth ultimately leads to snarling fights about water. Maybe our psyches won't allow us to hold that truth. We are animals, after all, with instincts to procreate, and although we have set aside many of our natural instincts—the ones that allow us to see ourselves as part of nature instead of nature's managers, for instance—we apparently cannot set aside the instinct, or religious mandate, to reproduce. We may not be capable of voluntarily shrinking our population to live within our natural means. Our instinct for individual creation obviously overrides our instinct—assuming we have one—for preservation of the whole, so maybe we simply continue down that road until we can go no farther. Our grandchildren might be okay; they might have some road still to travel. Their grandchildren may run out of road, but we don't even know them. Our great-great-grandchildren are hypothetical—we can't *feel* them—which makes our compassion for them equally hypothetical.

I live in and hike the canyons of Grand Staircase-Escalante National Monument, and when I drop off slickrock into a deep ravine such as Death Hollow to find mossy-walled springs, tall grasses, and tangled vines of poison ivy lining the creek, the tranquility that enters my body cannot be shrugged off as a luxury. I *need* water, not only to quench my thirst but to feed the anima of my being. That cannot happen without encountering water in its natural state, something we are quickly losing. If I follow the creek down Death Hollow, it will take me to the natural confluence with the Escalante River. If I follow the Escalante River, it will *not* take me to the Colorado River as it naturally should. How far can one travel on any western creek or river before butting up against a water project?

My body provides the mechanics of my life, but it does not operate independently of spirit. They are inseparable. I'm not emotionally or psychologically prepared for a world where all water is captured solely for survival of the body. Each summer

I make several trips to Upper Calf Creek Falls to swim in natural water, and each summer the number of people doing the same increases, possibly desperate for one chance at a disappearing opportunity. Their faces reflect sheer joy and wonder, emotions common when the physical body is immersed in its natural habitat. What happens when this is no longer possible? What if, in our cleverness, we find a way to physically survive without places like Death Hollow? Say we tap all sources of water the moment—or better still, before—they spring from the earth or run from the snowbank, and collect and store them for physical human survival as our western populations continue to grow? What happens to a species that carries a genetic imprint of nature when we pervert nature, when children can no longer splash in a creek?

I don't know the answer to that question, but it seems we are determined to find out. My gut feeling is that we lose an essential part of ourselves, the balancing part of humanity, the part that allows us peace despite fear, and joy amid sadness. The only part that allows us to love one another.

DIRT FANTASIES

*I bequeath myself to the dirt to grow
from the grass I love,
If you want me again look for me
under your boot-soles.*

—Walt Whitman

I dream about digging in dirt. In my fertile imagination dirt begins at sensuality, climbs the trellis of eroticism, and drops into the hole of debauchery where it romps lasciviously before climaxing in rebellious abandon.

Gorgeous, sexy people dig in dirt. People who age well. People who collect beauty in the creases of crow's-feet. People with sturdy hands and good minds. In the evenings, dirt diggers dine at friend-encircled tables, where laughter and wine pour forth in equal measure, where confident, unjeweled fingers twirl glasses, where dirt persists under nails and in cuticles. The diggers taste their food with more intensity, more essence than the nondiggers. The word "luscious" comes to mind.

I've been digging in dirt all day, they say, and then, *I love digging in dirt.* The words enter the atmosphere with such lustiness you quiver with images of black, loose dirt fondling your own fingers. And the dirt... oh, the dirt! So perfectly textured, like silk drawn over erect nipples. The dirt collects heat from the sun and offers it to you. But then, as you reach for it, the dirt playfully tugs you into its cool recesses. You're surprised when a barely audible moan spills from your lips.

Dirt fantasies, like sexual fantasies, vibrate with tension between imagination and reality. Both are genuine, and one plays off the other, gently correcting and merging the romance with the banal, the wild with the tame, the unconscious connection to dirt with the conscious experience of dirt.

The dirt surrounding my desert home is not perfectly textured. It is not rich and dark and moist and soft and cool to the touch. It does not gently stroke my arthritic fingers. It is not being aerated by slow-moving, benign worms. My dirt is dry, hot, hard-packed clay occupied by copious members of the family Formicidae—the industrious ant—which explore the giant in their midst by biting, ascertaining, I assume, my suitability as a food source and the possibility of carrying me away crumb by crumb. I try to cultivate a gentle attitude toward ants because I'm a fan of E. O. Wilson. I know ants are busy cultivating my claylike earth where worms fear to tread, but instead of dropping to my knees, lowering my face to the ground, and offering thanks, I swear and stomp at them. "Stop biting me, you little bastards!" I scream.

Ants are dirt-fantasy killers. Earwigs too. Flies also. Along with whatever gopher-type animal leaves loose dirt mounds— an impressive feat—on the surface of my small plot of solid earth. All these busy creatures share my dirt and outnumber me by maybe a million to one. They also share the products of my dirt, which is, I suppose, only fair. The legal authority proclaiming the dirt mine doesn't hold much sway with them.

Although my dirt is not the dirt of my dreams, it has taught me this: dirt does not need to achieve my idea of perfection to produce. Out of my broken clods of clay sprout tomatoes, squash, corn, peppers, and whatever else I manage to shove into the ground. Apples, pears, cherries, peaches, apricots, and plums drop onto concrete-like earth in my backyard year after year. Greenery breaks through also, a few blades of grass but mostly weeds that we mow and call "green space." I've been told I need to bring in "good soil" and work it into my dirt. That would certainly feed my fantasy, but there's something about the toughness of my dirt, and its ability to create new life in its current state, that keeps me from doing so. It seems a betrayal, like the sixty-year-old husband replacing his sixty-year-old wife with a younger woman, one smoother to the touch.

My vision of myself as a dirt digger is akin to that of the "avid hiker" with the never-worn expensive Italian hiking boots occupying a dark corner of the closet. Gardening is not my strong suit. I cram vegetable plants into my dirt—invariably too close to one another—and let them fend for themselves among the weeds. And they do. They hold strong. My garden is not suitable for the pages of a glossy magazine—it is an entangled mess that requires bravery and a machete to harvest—but it is hardy.

Still, my dirt fantasies remain intact. They are not frivolous. They are not based solely in romanticism, but I've come to realize that I'm not so much a dirt digger as I am a dirt wallower. Wet or dry, I love dirt on my skin.

My first recognition of this came in the summer of 1962 before I started first grade. A friend and I were playing on the cut, clean grass of my backyard, separated from the ditch behind it by an easily scalable chain link fence. The ditch was irresistible to me as were its banks made of soaked, claylike earth, which perplexed my mother. She had no concerns about me drowning; she fretted that I would track mud into the house and draw the ire of my father. My mother found yelling and swearing disturbing; my father found it an efficient way to communicate with his children.

As much as I loved my mother and feared my father, I needed that mud. I had never heard of women going to spas for mud treatments—I had never heard of spas—but the thought of cool, globby mud slathered on my skin may have been my first tingle, my first grab at forbidden fruit.

My friend and I spent some time in an excited state of indecision, edging toward the sin like two first-time adulterers. In the end, we settled on what we thought to be a brilliant compromise. The next-door neighbor boy, a year younger than us, had set up a classroom of stuffed animals and was in the process of dressing down a giant giraffe that had spoken out of turn. Because we were older and he was lonely, we made quick work of convincing him to sacrifice the giraffe to our cause. We would slop mud on the long-necked beast and cool ourselves in the process.

Why we thought this would lead to less trouble than slapping mud directly on our own skin is no longer part of my memory. As we would later find out from the boy's red-faced, furious mother, giant stuffed giraffes don't grow on trees, are nonwashable, and are meant to live indoors. Even though the giraffe was outdoors before its spa treatment began, that technicality didn't save us. Nevertheless, the superb idea first generated hours of reckless, muddy fun and shoved me down a lifelong path of dirt wallowing from which I would never recover.

In his book *Magical Child*, Joseph Chilton Pearce identifies the living earth as the second bonding matrix—after the mother—in a child's intellectual development. A child has no capacity for abstract explanations—the kind parents love to impart—of the world; her development is 100 percent experiential: mud feels good, doesn't taste good. Lesson learned. What else offers unqualified practicality but the natural world? If a child is unable to process the natural world through the body, says Pearce—rolling in sand and grass, eating dirt, chewing on sticks, sniffing flowers and dung, hearing the buzz of insects and birdsong—the patterns for practical sensory organization never form in that child's brain, and the creative logic of that child is forever thwarted.

My mother's purpose for sending me outdoors to play had little to do with her desire to create a magical child and more to do with her desire for silence, but despite her intentions, I found my place along the ditch banks and in the mud sloughs of the world.

I now leave stuffed animals out of my filthy activities—to this day I have disdain for their uselessness—but the urge to cover my skin in dirt has never left me. Desert quicksand after a monsoon provides a fleeting fix, but one can't typically get more than shin deep in it. If you know where to look, though, you can get your fix.

On a recent backpack, Steve and I camped at Fence Canyon along the Escalante River, walked upriver a mile or so where we were unlikely to see others, stripped down, and covered ourselves with mud from the riverbank. We then lay on our backs in the sun to crackle and dry, a sensual, full-body experience. Shortly after that, we heard about a natural hot spring/mud bath in a meadow near a small California town, and we drove six hours to sink ourselves into silky, black, sulfur-stinking mud. I can't imagine anyone not wanting the experience, but when I tell friends about it, they crinkle their noses and seldom ask for directions.

On my fiftieth birthday, Steve and I hiked to Boucher Creek at the west end of the Grand Canyon. The trail was harsh, the packs were heavy with extra water, and the temperature hovered around 110 degrees even though we had set out at 4:00 a.m. In the ranger's office the day before, we had been appraised under doubtful eyebrows, received a reluctant nod of approval, and were told we were on our own. Boucher Creek was difficult to reach, no other campers would be there, and no rangers would be coming to check on us. In other words, perfect conditions. The ranger warned us to be off the Tonto Plateau—referred to as "the death zone"—before 10:00 a.m., and we took his advice seriously. At 10:15, we dropped into Boucher Creek hot, dehydrated, and exhausted, stripped our bodies of packs and clothing, and lay on our backs on a flat rock in the creek, the tops of our heads acting as a sort of stop log to divert water around us.

For the next few days, we lived as close to the earth as modern humans from an unnatural civilization can live. We wore only a pair of sandals, sprawled in dirt, rinsed under waterfalls, swam in pools, and dried out on rocks. Unless submerged in water, we were never without dirt on our skin. We pressed our bodies together often, finding pleasure in the grit and heat between us. Four days later, when it came time to hike out, we reclothed ourselves in the items we had worn in. Nylon shorts and lightweight, sweat-wicking shirts felt heavy and restrictive—even somewhat silly. We spoke little on the hike out, silenced by the sanctity of the experience and the sadness of its rarity. I felt as if I came out of Boucher Creek in a stronger body, but it had nothing to do with physical strength. A more accurate description: I came out of Boucher Creek more strongly embodied.

Since that trip, we have sought such encounters. Sometimes for days, sometimes for only an afternoon, we shed our so-called protective layer and put body and earth together. A spiritual retreat within a natural retreat center. The longer the exposure to dirt, the more firmly embodied one becomes.

It is not unusual for humans to feel an impulse to shed clothing in the desert. It might be one of the most common surges of animal instinct remaining in us. In his book *The Man Who Walked Through Time*, Colin Fletcher writes about experiencing a heightened awareness upon removing his clothing, a more intimate consciousness of the interconnected web of life in the Grand Canyon. Without clothing he felt more physically a part of the interwoven ecosystem, and he felt more deeply the diminutiveness of the human time scale. I'm never surprised when I come upon naked people in the desert; I'm surprised it doesn't happen more frequently.

Without having conscious awareness of it, which is as it should be according to Pearce, I came out of childhood with a profound bond to dirt and carried that relationship into my adolescence. There, I found the charcoal-gray dirt of the Oquirrh Mountains near my childhood home, hard-packed with an inch or two of loosely floating topsoil that produced puffs of smoky dust when walked on. The barefoot hippie symbol of freedom reached my small town in the late '60s, a fad I enthusiastically embraced, partly because it mortified my mother and angered my father, but mostly because the human foot seemed then— and still seems now—a well-suited instrument for walking upon the earth, especially those parts of earth not covered by pavement and concrete. In short, it felt good. I still don't understand why the bare foot is repulsive to so many, why it's okay to track dirt into a store or restaurant on Vibram soles but not on the sole of the human foot.

A vision of my feet covered in the silt of the Oquirrhs is one of the most vivid memories I carry, and that memory is solidly attached to me. By that, I mean, there has always been a small place in me that yearns for my own life—the life I want to live versus the life I'm supposed to live. The supposed-to life fits neatly into the expectations of family and society; the want-to life departs drastically from that picture. The two can never fully merge because the want-to life includes a small house and the supposed-to life demands that I pay for it. But my interior place of craving remains, and it is solidly connected to the earth's surface. Somehow, putting the human body in direct contact with the earth infuses it with unrestrained imagination. I've carried this knowledge with me since childhood, albeit mostly at an unconscious level. Once I moved it into consciousness, I've stayed close to dirt and moved steadily toward the want-to life, disappointing many along the way, but pleasing the wistful girl sitting on a creek bank staring at her dirt-covered feet.

The older I get, the more essential dirt wallowing becomes. It reminds me that I can age, my stomach can lose its tautness, my skin can loosen, my joints can stiffen, and my body can begin to wear out as it is designed to do, but until it drops, it is still my body. It is the same body that forty-five years ago enjoyed a pair of Levi 501s drooping on its bare hips below its flat belly; the same body that has forever objected to the idea of being strapped into women's wear; the same body that soaked up too much sun, turned scarlet, and shed its outer layer of skin; and the same body that kicked up puffs of gray dust around bulging tree roots in the Oquirrh Mountains.

It is the dirt on the body that reminds it of its sensuality, that allows it to claim its carnal appetite at any age. In a culture where only young women are allowed to express themselves as sexual beings, dirt on the body allows the old woman to say: Fuck that. You don't determine my sexuality. I do. The earth does.

DARK LOVE

In a dark time, the eye begins to see.

—Theodore Roethke

It slips in quietly. A hint of terseness marks his voice, an opaque film covers his blue eyes, his face flushes and its lines deepen. His six-foot-four frame droops toward the floor as if he's ashamed to drape his sorry self over it, and he tries to creep from the room unnoticed. It hurts him to be seen.

We share the only bed in our house, but he curls close to the edge, his face in the moonlight twisted and consternated. I want to reach out with a soothing touch, but I have learned not to. When he is deep in his dark world, a simple touch will send a startle response through his bones. He will burst from the bed as if facing a knife-wielding attacker and his wild eyes will be locked on me.

When I wake in the morning to find his side of the bed cold, I search for signs: a spoon in the sink indicates coffee was made; a creaking floor in his upstairs office indicates movement. From the signs, I can measure the depth of his depression and the probable length of its stay. No signs at all, and I feel as if I've been stalked into a dead-end alley.

I once believed myself capable of empathetic greatness, a belief that's been gutted and redesigned like a nineteenth-century farmhouse. The crumbling bricks still hold, but the interior structure bears little resemblance to the original.

Steve was fifty when we met; I was forty-eight. Our future held no golden wedding anniversary; silver was dubious. Such reckonings cut short the discovery period of romance enjoyed by the young. We acknowledged our love for each other, and, almost in the same breath, we acknowledged our impediments: Steve's depression, my anxiety.

Having anxiety in our anxious culture is like wearing a white T-shirt—it's not conspicuous—so I had minimal awareness of its scope. And being wholly naive about depression, I shrugged it off in the name of love. With less caution than warranted, Steve and I joined hands and stepped into the abyss.

Anxiety and depression share commonalities. In our case, the emotional memories of each are decades—maybe generations—old, with no faces, no bodies, no specific points of origin. The similarities generate compassion between us but not necessarily understanding. And distinct differences make us ill-suited for sharing a life.

Anxiety gushes out, soliciting reassurance and relief; depression pulls in and sets up barriers. Anxious people want to process, often in a desperate, frenetic way. But insisting that a depressed person process his current state is worse than futile; it is merciless. Working together, depression and anxiety construct a near-impermeable trap. When I sense Steve's depression, I churn in angst. When Steve senses my anxiety, he drops deeper.

Steve's depression is episodic, triggered in a moment that takes him down. And in that moment, life is brusquely shifted, shut down for an indefinable period. When I first saw it, although I had been forewarned, I had no idea what I was seeing. The shift in physical appearance alone pulled me up short, and the abrupt change in personality seemed like a subterfuge. And for many years I treated it as such, demanding that he stop and explain himself.

He retreats into his impenetrable misery behind the closed door of his office. I walk to keep my body occupied while my emotions lurch from confusion to sadness to anger to desperation. I return to a quiet house, no traces of movement. I search the bookshelves and Internet for comfort. So much advice—all of it familiar, none of it useful. Two days go by without verification of life. I stew and listen and watch. I dissect the days and hours leading up to the moment it slithered in. I pinpoint the trigger and rewrite the script. I chant a whispered mantra: "This will end." But I worry that it won't end, that we'll be here on our respective sides of a cheap, hollow door three weeks, three months, three years from now.

On the third day, the door opens and I jump to attention. He slouches down the stairs without making eye contact, looking ten years older than he looked four days prior. I offer to make soup, I suggest a hike, I extend bookshelf advice in a cheerful voice tinged with urgency. I speak to him as if he doesn't understand his own mind. He goes back upstairs and shuts the door.

Steve embodies light and dark in their extremities. The dark runs deep and murky, but radical light runs parallel. I fear the dark will snuff out the light and destroy him, destroy us. He assures me that will never happen, and like a religious skeptic teetering on the edges, I work to keep the faith.

I want to pry him apart, separate light from dark. I want the model with the personalized options, not the package deal, but his GPS is already installed. Ripping it out would leave him lighter, yes, but also deformed, shrunken, misshapen. Much of his beauty comes out of the shadow. His gentleness, his patience, his wisdom, his passion—all flow from having dwelt in the tender place of despair. I deeply understand the truth of this. Still, I want it to be easier—for him, yes, but mostly for me. He knows this darkness, and he oddly draws strength from its familiarity, as if it constitutes some sort of sacred ritual. I cower in its presence.

On the fourth day, I wake to find the office door open and him gone. I breathe a sigh of relief for a morning without his dark presence and say a small prayer to the gods he worships: red rock canyons and sagebrush flats. He has gone to the desert.

I walk out to the garage to see what's not there: a cot, a sleeping bag, a five-gallon water jug. All good signs. He will spend nights under a dark sky, and when the sun rouses him, he will walk between red rock walls, bumping against them in his rawness. He will find a flat run of slickrock to lie upon, and he will stay until desert light finds a fissure in his constructed shield. Then he'll come back to me.

Shortly after I met him, Steve said something that would become a refrain in our relationship: "I need to go to the desert." We met in Tucson and lived in Salt Lake City, so technically we had always been in a desert, but that's not what he meant. He sought a desert free of humans and their debris, full of light, where he could dwell undisturbed for an extended period.

Having grown up in Utah's west desert, I, too, have an appreciation for such places, but I initially thought him prone to hyperbole. Imprudently clinging to the popular view that all power lies within, I equated Steve's stated need to the exaggerated notions of a teenager needing a new iPhone. But after thirteen years of inadvertent research, my flippancy has waned.

On our wedding day, Steve promised to always rescue himself—it was written into the vows. In my most anxious moments,

I have extracted the promise from him again and again, but the last time I did was in the autumn of 2013, which was when I, at long last, understood that he has only one fail-safe rescue: the desert.

It was our worst year together, high anxiety and deep depression, each tightening the knots of the other. We futilely tugged from opposite ends for eight months. In the fall, I suggested a weekend backpack on the Escalante River, and he nodded his agreement. But on the day we were supposed to leave, he couldn't rally the energy to abide my company, having, no doubt, sensed my desperate reach for relief. After he shut the upstairs door, I sat amid the mess of freeze-dried food packets and cried. Then I packed.

I would like to say I left the house quietly, but I didn't. I breached the sanctity of the closed door and made a dramatic, sobbing speech and exit. I no longer remember the words, but I remember the cruelty behind them. I'm sure I demanded some sort of promise or explanation that he could not possibly give. I remember his horrified face as I loaded my pain onto his.

I drove fifteen miles to the trailhead shaking with the kind of generalized rage that has no receptacle. Only after hoisting the pack and splashing through the knee-high, sun-warmed water for the first of many river crossings did I acknowledge that I had never backpacked alone, never spent a night *out there* by myself. It was an easy three-mile hike upriver to the Sand Creek confluence where I planned to camp, and the physical risk was minimal. But the sun drops early in the river gorge, and the long stretch of night ahead played on my nerves.

Righteous indignation propelled me forward, a feeling of something having been thrust upon me that I did not deserve. I slogged through deep sand, stumbled often, and expended a great deal of energy to gain little ground. Had I lifted my eyes from the trail, I might have been awed by Escalante Natural Bridge, a sturdy, flat-topped, deep red and brown arch that spans a side canyon like a train trestle. Had I lifted my eyes, my heart may have been lightened—or at least distracted—by the Indian domicile ruins on a ledge next to a wall of seven-hundred-year-old petroglyphs. But I did not lift my eyes. I rounded the bend in the river that alerted me to the confluence without acknowledging the painted red snake on the slickrock I skirted, without pondering its symbolism, although it may have been as relevant to me as it was to its creator. Rebirth? Resurrection? Initiation?

I dropped into a hole that brought the river to my upper thighs before climbing the sandy, steep bank on hands and knees. Knowing that seeking ant-free ground would be futile, I pitched my tent among the small creatures under a cluster of cottonwoods and cooked dinner before the sun went down. Then I crossed the cold, shin-high waters of Sand Creek and set my Thermarest chair on a partially dry, flat rock in the last splice of sunlight. I faced a soaring, creamsicle-orange wall with white streaks—as if someone had poured a bucket of Clorox from the top every few yards—and waited for darkness to descend. But it never did.

The wall, a magnificent domed rock bestowed with runs of creamy smoothness from calving, was the last in the canyon to lose light. It presided over the celestial ceremony of sundown—quieting the whistling birds, hushing the croaking ravens, piloting a change of temperature and a kettle of turkey vultures on a gust. As the diurnal fell silent, whispering grasses and rustling river willows filled the void. On my right, a tranquil spring wallpapered the Navajo sandstone with ivy, ferns, and columbine before trickling through a crack in many straggling fountains at mouth level and leaving the rocks below it covered in spongy lime-green moss.

Sand Creek approached me from behind a grassy bend, ran over slickrock and sand, bumped against, and parted for, volcanic boulders, passed me close enough to splash my left arm and leg, gathered spring water from the right, and then disappeared around an eastern bend to meet the river. Near and distant, peach and rose, honey- and ginger-colored walls, polished to a high sheen by desert varnish and pockmarked by wind and water, surrounded me on all sides, sharing the waning warmth of the sun.

As the reigning wall lost its light, the hanging garden lost its shimmer in the shadows, the creek gurgled, the spring trickled, and a warm breeze blew. I sat very still, every sense heightened—and pacified. Tranquility edged in like rainwater through a crack in sandstone. After a while, I could no longer discern my feet on the rock or sand on my skin. The place integrated my presence as if I were natural to it, and I felt the whole of it.

I sat. I had been breathing shallowly for many months, holding myself together with a pinched brow and rigid muscles. I breathed. My shoulders fell. Fear and dread oozed from my body and was cleanly washed away by Sand Creek—as if it were no problem at all—and delivered to the river where it would flow out of reach. *Shhhh,* the place whispered. *Be still.*

Moonlight climbed sandstone walls bringing with it the thought of Steve's refrain: "I need to go to the desert." I had heard the urgency in his voice, but I refused to hear the truth in his words. I had scoffed at the idea that a place could do for him what I could not—that a place could hold him, soothe him, reach into the depths of that darkness and pull him out. And now, here I sat, held by the place. And here was the thing that left me dumbfounded: the place had been here all along. Through many months of homebound angst, through my desperation and rage, through my vain perseverance, the place was here—flowing, buzzing, being.

That night on the slickrock bank of Sand Creek, I clearly understood what I had been doing to Steve for thirteen years. I had done what every well-meaning person in his life—every lover, every friend—had done. I had tried to *fix* him. And in doing so, I had delivered a sharp message: "I cannot love you this way."

The next morning, I was sitting on a log, swiping ants off my legs and sipping a cup of tea, when Steve walked into camp. He was not entirely tall and steady, but he was upright. He smiled weakly but genuinely, and I thought if ever there were an element natural in its desert environment, there it stands.

We walked up Sand Creek without conversation, each sensitive to the other's fragility. When we reached a sandy beach on the water's edge, we sat facing a hollowed-out red wall. "I have a gift for you," I said. He turned toward me, blue eyes tired but clear. I told him I would no longer participate in his depression; I would no longer view it as a problem to be fixed. "I am giving you the gift of your own depression," I told him. He looked at me for a long moment, and when he started breathing again, vestiges of apprehension drained from his face. "Thank you," he said.

I have since kept my promise. It turns out, I can love the whole of him, and doing so has settled something in me. I don't hold any notion that he will one day be cured of depression, and I no longer seek that. But removing myself as custodian of his state of being has given us space without shame. The chasm is shallower, more light filters in. In turn, I am released from my own shaking hellhole of onus and distress.

And then there's the desert, right here, where it's always been—gushing, illuminating, revealing.